Mammals

S0-ABM-703

If you have ever seen a dog, cat, mouse, or cow, or looked at yourself in a mirror, you have seen a mammal. Mammals come in many shapes and sizes. All mammals, however, share special traits.

Mammals are the only animals that nurse their young. This means that the babies are fed with the mother's milk.

Mammals are often very caring parents. They protect and train their young. One or both parents care for the babies. The young learn mostly by imitating, or copying, their parents.

Mammals are warm-blooded. Their body temperature stays about the same even though the air temperature around them changes.

All mammals have hair at some time in their lives. In some whales, though, hair is present only before birth.

Finally, mammals have larger, more complex brains than other animals. They are thought to be the most intelligent of all animals.

Write the answer to each question.

1. What do mammals feed their newborn babies?

_____

2. Who cares for the baby mammals?

_____

3. Young mammals imitate their parents. What does *imitate* mean?

_____

4. Mammals are warm-blooded. What does this mean? _____

_____

_____

5. Name two mammals. _____

Try This! On the back of this paper, list five ways mammals differ from other creatures.

FS-32049 Science

Natural Habitats of Mammals

Animals live in many kinds of surroundings. The place where an animal lives in nature is called its natural habitat. There are many kinds of natural habitats. Each animal is best suited to the habitat in which it lives.

The **ocean** is the watery home of whales, dolphins, porpoises, and seals. Elephants, lions, giraffes, and zebras live in grassy plains called **grasslands**. Mammals that live in the **forest** include wolves, bears, deer, and raccoons. Polar bears, arctic hares, caribou, and musk oxen live in the cold climate of the **polar regions**.

1. List each mammal under its natural habitat.

bear	zebra	caribou	lion
musk ox	dolphin	raccoon	wolf
porpoise	whale	polar bear	seal
elephant	arctic hare	giraffe	deer

Ocean	**Grasslands**	**Forest**	**Polar Regions**
_____	_____	_____	_____
_____	_____	_____	_____
_____	_____	_____	_____
_____	_____	_____	_____

2. Draw a picture showing one of the above animals in its natural habitat.

Try This! The desert is another habitat. List four animals that live there.

FS-32049 Science

The Blue Whale

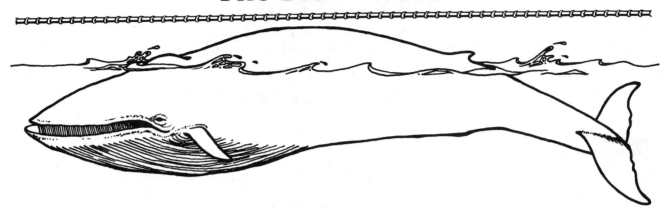

The blue whale is the largest animal in the world. It is a sea mammal. It can grow up to 100 feet long and weigh as much as 100 tons.

Unlike most mammals which have four legs, the blue whale does not have any legs. Instead, it has two front flippers. It uses its flippers for steering and balancing while swimming.

The blue whale has no teeth. Instead, it has thin plates, called baleen, that hang from the roof of its mouth. The baleen looks like the teeth of a comb and acts as a strainer. When the blue whale eats, it opens its huge mouth and takes in large amounts of water and krill, a tiny shrimplike animal. The water is then forced out through the baleen and the krill is left behind to be swallowed.

Write the answer to each question.

1. What is the length and weight of a blue whale?

   _____

2. What does the blue whale use its flippers for while it is swimming?

   _____

3. What hangs from the roof of the blue whale's mouth?

   _____

4. What does the blue whale eat? _____

5. Can blue whales chew food? _____

Try This! Write five more facts about the blue whale. A library book or encyclopedia will help you.

FS-32049 Science

Mammal Hunt

Use the pictures to help you write the answers to the riddles.

blue whale

beaver

bat

horse

anteater

elephant

monkey

camel

1. I have a hump on my back that I use for storing fat.

   _____

2. I live in the ocean. I am the largest of all mammals.

   _____

3. I am the only flying mammal. _____

4. I have a long snout and sticky tongue. I mainly eat ants.

   _____

5. I use my sharp front teeth to cut down trees. My broad, flat tail looks like a paddle. _____

6. I am the largest land mammal. I have a trunk and tusks.

   _____

7. My fingers help me hold things. I like to swing from tree branches.

   _____

8. I sometimes wear "shoes." I provide transportation and pleasure for many people. _____

Try This! Write a riddle about another mammal. Trade with a friend.

4

Animal Behavior

The behavior of an animal is the way in which the animal acts. There are two types of animal behavior.

Instinct is behavior that the animal knows from birth. It is behavior that the animal does automatically without thinking about it. A bird building a nest, for example, acts from instinct. No one had to teach the bird what to do.

Learned behavior is something that an animal learns to do. It is behavior that an animal would not do naturally. For example, a circus seal that balances a ball on its nose does so because someone taught it to do the trick. Balancing a ball is not part of the seal's natural behavior.

Write each phrase under the correct heading.

- a bird feeding her young
- a bear hibernating in winter
- a horse performing in a horse show
- a skunk spraying in danger
- a dog catching a stick
- a porpoise jumping through a hoop

Instinct	**Learned Behavior**
1. _____	1. _____
_____	_____
2. _____	2. _____
_____	_____
3. _____	3. _____

Try This! If you could teach an animal to do a trick, which animal would you choose and what would the trick be? Write your answer.

5   FS-32049 Science

Mammal Communication

Mammals can communicate. Although they do not talk as people do, they share information. Mammals are born knowing how to communicate with mammals of their own kind.

Some mammals use sound signals to communicate. Dogs and wolves bark. Lions use low coughs. Chimpanzees make sounds that have specific meanings. Prairie dogs whistle to warn one another of danger.

Scent is another way mammals communicate. A bear, for example, leaves its scent around its territory by plastering mud on trees and rubbing its back against the mud. Its hairs rub off and leave a scent indicating the bear's presence.

Some mammals communicate with their face and body. Wolves draw back their upper lip and show their fangs when in danger. Gorillas beat their chest with their fists when they are angry.

Touch is another form of animal communication. Horses, deer, and cattle show affection by nuzzling, licking, and neck rubbing. Chimpanzees sometimes hug to show affection.

Circle **True** or **False** for each statement below.

1. Some mammals use sound signals to communicate.   True   False
2. Mammals must be taught how to communicate.   True   False
3. Bears communicate using scent messages.   True   False
4. A wolf's face changes when it senses danger.   True   False
5. No mammal communicates by touching.   True   False
6. Gorillas sometimes show they are angry.   True   False
7. Horses never show affection.   True   False
8. Prairie dogs whistle when there is danger.   True   False

Try This! Write three ways that a dog or cat can communicate with its owner.

Mammal Report

Choose a mammal for your report.
Complete the sentences.

1. The title of this report is _____

2. The mammal I am reporting on is _____

3. This mammal lives _____

   _____

   _____

4. This mammal has _____

   _____

5. This mammal eats _____

   _____

6. This mammal likes to _____

   _____

   _____

7. This mammal can _____

   _____

8. The information for this report came from _____

   _____

   _____

Try This! Draw a picture of the mammal in your report on the back
of this sheet.

7

Mammal Observation Sheet

Observe means to watch or study. Select a mammal to observe. Observe your mammal at different times of the day. Try to find out how it eats and sleeps. Write your observations on the lines below.

1. The animal I observed was a _____

2. The place where I observed the animal was _____
    _____

3. The animal I observed did the following:

    In the morning _____
    _____

    Around noontime _____
    _____

    In the afternoon _____
    _____

4. This is how the animal moved: _____
    _____
    _____

5. This animal ate _____
    _____

6. The noises that this animal made were _____
    _____

7. The animal slept _____
    _____

Try This! Write a paragraph describing the animal you observed.

What Is a Bird?

A bird is an animal with feathers. Feathers protect a bird's skin and help it keep warm. Feathers also help to waterproof a bird's body.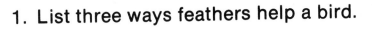

A bird has two legs and a hard beak. It also has many bones that are hollow like a straw. These bones make the bird lighter and better able to fly. Some birds such as the penguin, though, cannot fly.

Every bird hatches from an egg. The egg is kept warm by the father or mother bird. When the young bird hatches, it is usually fed by its parents.

Write the answers.

1. List three ways feathers help a bird.

_____

_____

_____

2. How do hollow bones help birds?

_____

_____

3. Name one bird that cannot fly. _____

4. Who usually cares for a bird when it hatches?

_____

_____

5. What is your favorite bird? Why is it your favorite?

_____

_____

Try This! List as many birds as you can. Try to name at least ten.

9

Birds and Their Nests

Use words from the Word Box to fill in the blanks.

Word Box			
beaks	buildings	holes	lined
build	hatched	nests	sticks

eagle

Most birds build nests to hold their eggs and protect their young. Baby birds are hatched and fed in the nest.

robin

Robins, goldfinches, and sparrows make bowl-shaped nests called open nests. The nests are made of grass, twigs, and leaves, and 1._____ with mud.

Pigeons, eagles, and ospreys build stick nests. They build a platform of 2._____ and twigs high up in a tree or on a cliff.

flamingo

Many birds use mud to make nests. Flamingos use their 3._____ to scrape mud into a mound. Swallows 4._____ nests of mud mixed with straw and grass, and lined with feathers. You can find swallow nests on cliffs or attached to 5._____ .

woodpecker

Woodpeckers find old trees and use their beaks to make 6._____ for their nests. Chickadees, wrens, and owls use old woodpecker holes for their 7._____ .

The cowbird does not build a nest at all. Instead it lays its eggs in the nest of a smaller bird. The egg is 8._____ and raised by its "foster parents."

Try This! Birds know how to build nests by instinct. Name two things you can do that you did not have to learn.

FS-32049 Science

Bird Beaks

Birds use their beaks to eat, take care of their babies, build nests, and protect themselves.

1. A **grosbeak** has a very strong, cone-shaped beak which it uses for cracking seeds.

2. The **spoonbill** uses its spoon-shaped bill to sweep back and forth in water to find food.

3. A **woodpecker** hunts insects by drilling into trees with its thin, pointed beak.

4. The **golden eagle** has a hooked beak that it uses for tearing its prey.

5. The **brown creeper** uses its small, slender beak to search under bark for insects.

6. The beak of the **nighthawk** opens wide and traps insects in midair.

Using the clues from above, write the name of each bird under its picture.

A. _____

B. _____

C. _____

D. _____

E. _____

F. _____

Try This! Find and write four facts about one of the birds listed above.

Bird Feet

Birds have two feet to help them walk, hop, run, swim, climb, and perch. Each bird has the kind of feet best suited to its way of life.

The **grasping** feet of hawks, eagles, and owls have large, curved claws to snatch fish from water or to hold on to mice, toads, and lizards. The **scratching** feet of crows, chickens, turkeys, and quails are good for searching in the soil for grains and seeds.

Ducks, gulls, storks, and geese have **webbed** feet. These water birds use their feet like paddles for swimming and wading. The feet of killdeer, roadrunners, and ostriches are designed for **running**. Their toes have short claws and are very strong.

Wrens, sparrows, and finches have **perching** feet. Each foot has one hind toe and three front toes to help these songbirds grasp branches tightly. The **climbing** feet of woodpeckers, parrots, and creepers help them get a good grip on tree trunks as they climb up, down, or around.

List three birds for each kind of foot.

Climbing foot

_____
_____
_____

Scratching foot

_____
_____
_____

Webbed foot

_____
_____
_____

Grasping foot

_____
_____
_____

Running foot

_____
_____
_____

Perching foot

_____
_____
_____

Try This! Write about the kind of feet you would like to have if you were a bird.

12

Comparing Birds

The roadrunner lives in the deserts of western North America. The adult bird is twenty-three inches long and has brown and tan feathers. Its powerful beak can kill snakes and scorpions, but lizards are its main food. A roadrunner builds its nest in a cactus or bush. The female lays two to nine eggs at a time.

The ruby-throated hummingbird lives in eastern North America. It grows to be only three and one-half inches long. It uses its long, pointed beak to sip flower nectar, and catch insects and spiders. The mother hummingbird usually lays two, pea-sized, white eggs in a nest about the size of a quarter.

Write the phrases below under the correct heading.

- desert bird
- very small bird
- long, pointed beak
- powerful beak
- sips nectar
- eats lizards
- eastern North America
- western North America

Roadrunner

Ruby-throated Hummingbird

_____

_____

_____

_____

_____

_____

_____

_____

Try This! Compare two other North American birds. Write four phrases to describe each.

FS-32049 Science

State Birds

Phil was working on a report about state birds. In an almanac, he was surprised to find that many states had the same state bird. Here is a chart of some of the state birds that Phil learned about.

Bluebird - Idaho, New York, Nevada, Missouri	**Robin** - Michigan, Connecticut, Wisconsin
Goldfinch - New Jersey, Washington, Iowa	**Cardinal** - Illinois, Ohio, Kentucky, Indiana, North Carolina, Virginia, West Virginia
Chickadee - Maine, Massachusetts	

On the line beside each bird, write the number of states that have that bird as their state bird.

Goldfinch    Robin

_____   _____

Cardinal

_____

 Chickadee

_____   Bluebird

_____

Write the answers to the following questions.

1. What is the state bird of Maine? _____

2. How many states have the goldfinch as their state bird? _____

3. Which states have the bluebird as their state bird? _____

_____

4. How many states have the cardinal as their state bird? _____

5. What is the state bird of Wisconsin? _____

Try This! Paint a picture of your state bird.

14   FS-32049 Science

Bird Migration

Some birds like the blue jay, quail, and cardinal stay in one area all year long. But many birds migrate, or move from one place to another, when the seasons change. When the weather turns cold and food is hard to find, these birds fly south to warmer areas. When spring comes, they fly north again to build their nests.

Some birds migrate during the day, but many travel in the darkness of night for protection. Ducks, geese, hawks, and swallows migrate during the day, while timid songbirds such as warblers and thrushes travel at night.

Migration is full of dangers for the winged travelers. Often birds crash into high objects such as tall buildings or power lines. Sometimes birds fly into storms or strong winds and do not survive.

How do migrating birds find their way? Birds have an excellent sense of direction. Scientists think that birds may use the sun, stars, winds, or the shape of the land below to guide them.

Complete the sentences by filling in the missing letters.

1. When birds travel due to seasonal changes, it is called
   __ i __ __ a __ i o __ .

2. Many birds fly south when the __ e a __ __ e __ becomes cold.

3. Some birds use the darkness of night for
   __ __ o __ e __ __ i o __ .

4. Most songbirds travel at __ i __ __ __ .

5. Birds have a good sense of __ i __ e __ __ i o __ .

6. Migration is full of __ a __ __ e __ __ for birds.

7. Sometimes birds crash into tall __ u i __ __ i __ __ __ .

Try This! If you were a migrating bird, would you travel at night or during the day? Explain why.

FS-32049 Science

John James Audubon

John James Audubon was born on April 26, 1785. He was one of the first people to study and paint the birds of North America.

As a boy living in France he learned to hunt and to play the violin, but he preferred to go on hikes and collect birds' nests and eggs. Before he was 18, he had made about 200 drawings of birds.

In 1803 Audubon came to America. Later he married Lucy Bakewell. She believed that John was a great artist. She worked as a teacher to support the family. John traveled through the American countryside, watching, collecting, and painting birds.

Audubon's paintings were published in a book. They showed life-sized birds nesting, feeding, fighting, and flying. He mixed pencil, watercolor, crayon, chalk, and ink to make his birds look real.

Use the facts above to finish each sentence.

1. John Audubon _____

   _____

2. When John was young _____

   _____

3. In 1803 _____

   _____

4. Lucy believed _____

   _____

5. To make his paintings look real, John _____

   _____

6. Audubon's paintings _____

   _____

Try This! Write three questions you wish you could ask John James Audubon about his life.

Name _____

Our Atmosphere

All around our world is a thick layer of air. We call it our <u>atmosphere</u>. It is always changing. It can be hot or cold. It can be wet or dry. This changing is called <u>weather.</u>

Weather is caused by the sun. The sun causes wind, rain, clouds and snow.

Weather happens only in our layer of air. There is no weather in outer space.

Some places are dry most of the time. That is called a dry <u>climate.</u> Some places are wet most of the time. That is called a wet <u>climate.</u> If hot places have mountains, there could still be snow on the mountains. That is because the higher you climb the colder it gets.

Write the answers to the questions.

1. What is our layer of air called? _____

_____

2. What is the changing of our atmosphere called? _____

_____

3. What causes weather? _____

_____

4. Where is there no weather? _____

_____

Space

Atmosphere

Color the diagram using these colors.

Land—green   Atmosphere—white
Water—blue   Space—black

Let's Make a Book!

1. Begin looking for weather pictures in magazines and newspapers. Cut them out.

2. Start a file to keep all your weather papers.

3. Start a list of <u>Weather Words</u>. Copy the underlined words on your list.

4. Begin watching T.V. weather reports.

17

My Weather Chart for _____

Weather Symbols

| Clear | Cirrus | Cumulus | Stratus | Nimbus | Snow | Thunderstorm | Sleet | Fog or Smog |

S	M	T	W	Th	F	S

Number your chart to match your calendar.
Draw a weather symbol each day.

Name

Air Temperature

The <u>temperature</u> means how hot or cold something is. The earth gets heat from the sun. But the sun does not heat everything evenly. Some of the heat is soaked up by the atmosphere. Some of it goes into the earth. When the earth is warmed, it heats the air near it. Warm air rises. When this air goes up, cold air above comes down to fill up the gap the warm air left. This makes wind. This also changes the temperature.

Land soaks up and gives off heat quickly. But the oceans warm and give off heat slowly. All these things make temperature change.

We read <u>temperatures</u> on a thermometer. Read a thermometer at your home or school to see what the temperatures are in your town.

Write the answers to the questions.

1. _____ means how hot or cold something is.

2. From what do we get our heat? _____

3. Name two things that soak up the heat. _____

4. What soaks up the heat quickly? _____

5. From what do we read temperatures? _____

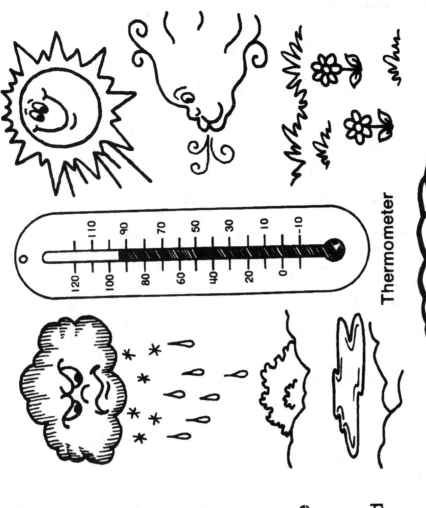

Thermometer

Let's Make a Book!

Draw a thermometer like the one shown.
Write a sentence or two under it, telling something about it.
Keep it for your book.

FS-32049 Science

Name _____

Air Pressure

Air is everywhere. Air is pushing against you all the time. You do not feel it because you have air inside of you, too! And this inside air is pushing out as hard as the outside air is pushing in. Lucky thing! Or you would be smashed flat!

Air, like everything else, is made of many small parts, called <u>molecules</u>. When air gets hot, it gets "bigger." Then these molecules spread out. They can't push as hard. We call this <u>low pressure</u>.

When air is cold it shrinks. Then the molecules are packed together. Now they push very hard! We call this <u>high pressure</u>.

Low pressure (or a "Low" on a weather map) brings bad weather. High pressure, or a "High," brings good weather.

Write the answers to the questions.

1. What is air doing all the time? _____

_____

2. Why don't you feel it? _____

_____

3. What is air made of? _____

4. What temperature causes low pressure? _____

5. What weather does a "High" bring? _____

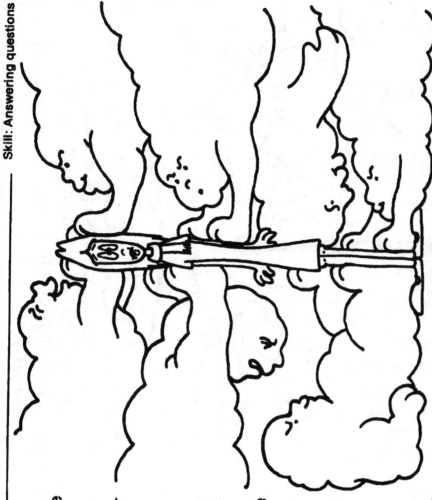

Let's Make a Book!

Do an experiment, then write about it for your book.

Put about ½ cup of water in a 2 gallon tin can. Heat until it steams. Remove from heat. Fit with <u>air-tight</u> lid. Allow can to cool. Watch to see what happens ...Why?

20

FS-32049 Science

Name _____

Super Water!

When you turn on the faucet, you get water. When you swim, you swim in water. When you sail in a boat, you ride on water. When it rains, that is water.

So you know what water is. Then what is an ice cube? That is water, too!

Water is not like you. It can change when the weather changes. You know water as a liquid. But when it gets very cold, liquid turns into a solid. We say it freezes. Ice is solid water.

When liquid water gets warm, it turns to a gas. (This is not like the gas you put in your car.) The air around you is gas. You cannot see it, but it is real. This water in the form of gas is called <u>water vapor.</u>

So water can be solid, liquid, or gas.

Write the answers to the questions.

1. How is water not like you? _____
_____
_____

2. When water gets very cold, it _____ .

3. When water gets warm, it _____ .

4. What is the air around you? _____

5. Water can be _____, _____ or _____

Find the solid, liquid and vapor water.

Let's Make a Book!

Fold a large paper in thirds. Draw pictures showing water in its three forms. Hint: Steam from something hot is water vapor. Label your pictures.

21

Name

How Clouds Form

Clouds are made of tiny drops of water and specks of dust. Some clouds are made of tiny bits of ice. These drops or bits are very tiny! More than 100 million could fit in a teaspoon!

The sun shines on the oceans, rivers and lakes. When the water is warmed, it is changed to a gas called water vapor. We say, "It <u>evaporated</u>."

Warm air always rises, so this vapor goes up. The upper air is cooler. Now the water vapor bumps into specks of dust that are cold.

It becomes liquid again. We say, "It <u>condenses</u>." Billions of these drops come together to form a cloud.

Write the answers to the questions.

1. What are clouds made of? _____

2. What sentence shows you how tiny they are? _____

3. When liquid water became vapor, it _____

4. Where does warm air always go? _____

5. When vapor becomes liquid, it _____

Let's Make a Book!

Do some Tear-Paste Art:

Needed: 12" x 18" blue paper
Scraps—all colors
Paste
No scissors!

FS-32049 Science

Name

Kinds of Clouds

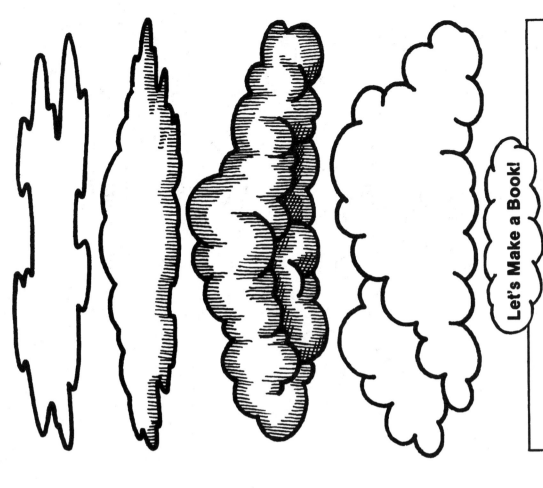

The fluffy white clouds you like to draw are cumulus clouds. They pile up like great balls of cotton. Cumulus means "pile." These clouds don't have a lot of water in them. They are "fair weather" clouds.

Nimbus clouds are very dark. They can be any shape. They bring lots of rain.

When the whole sky is covered in a blanket of gray, that's stratus clouds. If they are low, there will be a light rain called a drizzle.

Cirrus clouds are the highest in the sky. They can be 8–10 miles up in the sky. They look like wisps of smoke and are made of ice.

You can walk through the lowest cloud. We call it fog.

Let's Make a Book!

Find pictures of clouds. Some clouds are mixtures of these. Draw different clouds. Label them. Put them in your file for your book.

Write the answers to the questions.

1. What are the "fair weather" clouds? _____

2. What are the rain clouds? _____

3. What is like a gray blanket? _____

4. What is the highest cloud? _____

5. What is the lowest cloud? _____

23

Lay this page face down on the other half of the cloud chart on page 25.
Glue here.
Fold back on dotted line.

Name ______________________________ Skill: Drawing to scale

Glue other half of cloud chart here.
Fold it back.
Your chart will be 17 inches high.

CHART

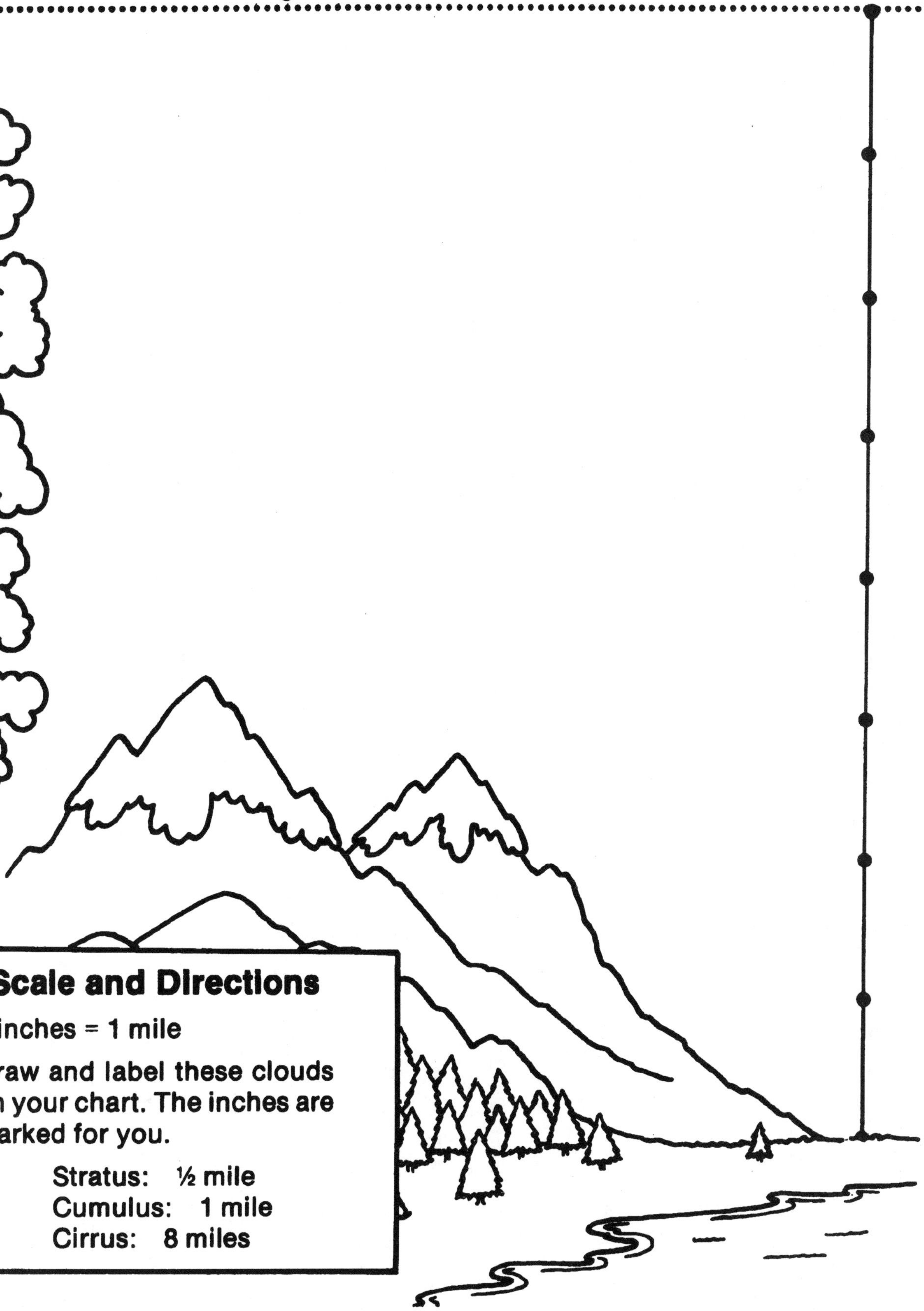

Scale and Directions

2 inches = 1 mile

Draw and label these clouds on your chart. The inches are marked for you.

Stratus: ½ mile
Cumulus: 1 mile
Cirrus: 8 miles

Name _____

Smog

Smog is a man-made kind of weather. Years ago it was unknown.

Smog is found hanging over many large cities of the world. The word "smog" is made of two words: smoke and fog.

Large cities have many industries. Industries give off smoke. Cities have many cars and buses. They give off exhaust.

When water evaporates, it collects and condenses on bits of dirt in the air. In large cities where the air is dirty, this makes smog.

Smog is a problem. It is bad for our eyes and lungs. We are always looking for ways to rid ourselves of smog.

Write answers to the questions.

1. Where is smog found? _____

_____

2. What two words make the word "smog"? _____

_____

3. What makes the smoke? _____

4. What does water vapor need to condense? _____

Let's Make a Book!

You are the mayor of a large, smoggy city. You must get rid of this problem. What is your plan? Write it down for your book.

FS-32049 Science

Name

The Water Cycle

The dark clouds begin to rain. The rain falls on the grass and the streets, making puddles. It falls on the hills, running down in little streams. They flow into lakes and on to the ocean.

The rain is over. Out peeks the sun. The water in the puddles, streams, lakes, and ocean gets warm. It changes to vapor, like steam rising out of a boiling teakettle. It disappears into the air.

Warm air rises, so up it goes. The air is cooler here. There are specks of dust. When the vapor hits a cool speck, it sticks to it and condenses. These bits of dust and water drops come together to make clouds. When they are heavy with water, down comes the rain again.

Do you see why it is called a cycle?

Write the answers to the questions.

1. What falls from the dark clouds? _____

2. What warms the water? _____

3. When water is warmed, what happens? _____

4. When vapor hits a cool speck, what does it do? _____

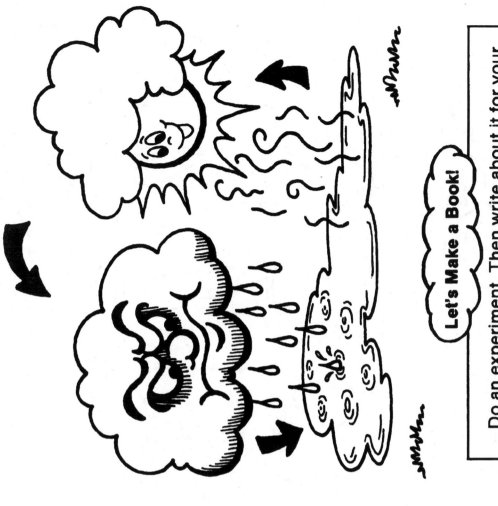

Let's Make a Book!

Do an experiment. Then write about it for your book:

Put a cup of water in a flat pan. Heat to boiling. Put ice cubes in a small pan. Hold it over the steam. Watch the water cycle!

Name

cut out

The Water Cycle Wheel

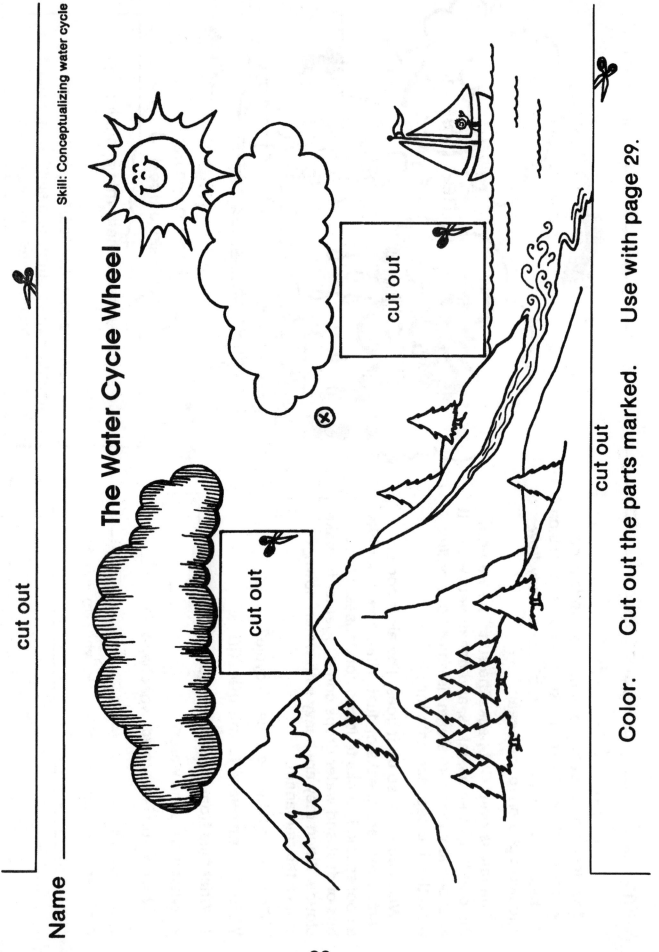

cut out

cut out

cut out

Color. Cut out the parts marked. Use with page 29.

FS-32049 Science

1. Color the water drops blue.

2. Cut out the circle.

3. Place the circle behind page 28.

4. Put a paper fastener through both ⊗.

5. Turn to see the water cycle.

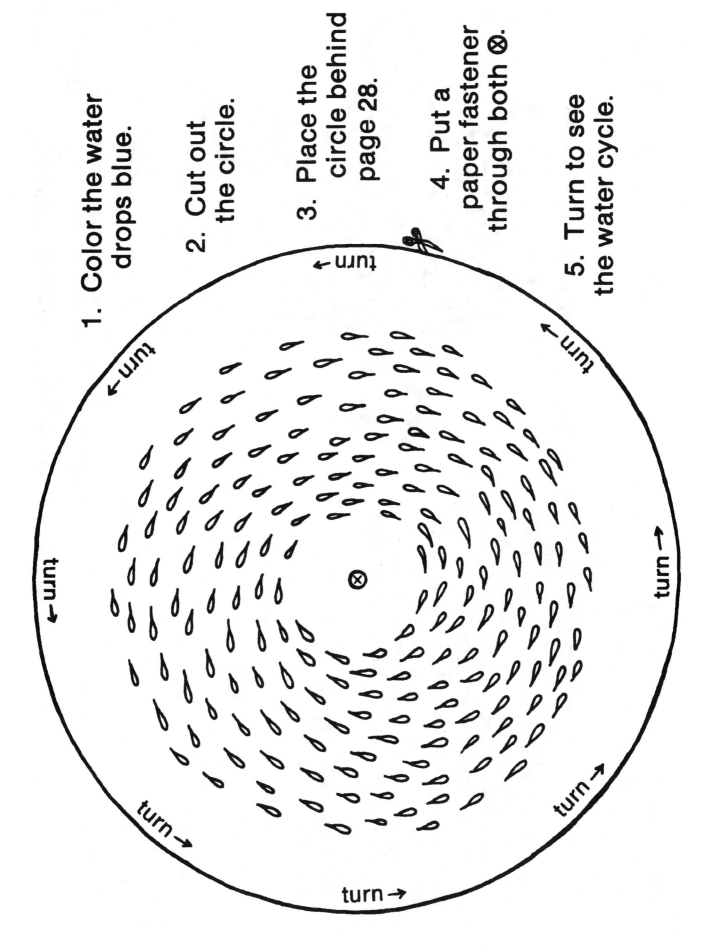

turn ←

turn ←

turn ←

turn ←

turn →

turn →

turn →

turn →

29

FS-32049 Science

Name _____

Rain and Snow

Clouds are made of billions of drops of water. When the drops grow very big and heavy, they fall as <u>rain.</u>

<u>Snow</u> is different. The weather does not have to be hot for water to evaporate. Evaporation can happen in cold winter weather. Snow does not have to melt to evaporate. Have you ever seen a patch of snow get smaller and smaller, yet the ground is dry?

The water vapor reaches the upper air layer where it is freezing. The vapor freezes, rather than condenses. Snow is frozen water vapor. Snow clouds are made of billions of flakes of frozen water vapor.

Let's Make a Book!

Follow the directions on "How to Cut a Snowflake." Cut out 3 or 4 different ones. Mount them on dark colored paper. Put them in your book.

Write the answers to the questions.

1. When does it rain? _____

_____

2. When can evaporation happen? _____

_____

3. What does the water vapor do? _____

4. What is snow? _____

5. What are snow clouds made of? _____

30   FS-32049 Science

How to Cut a Snowflake

All snowflakes have 6 sides. No two are alike!

1.
Start with a square.
(Rectangle works, too)

2.
Fold in half.

3.
Fold in half
again. Open
back to step 2.

4.
Fold left side to
center fold line.
Open back to step 2.

5.
Press finger at A.
Hold in place.

6.
Fold corner B
to touch line C.

7.
Fold up side D to line up
evenly with side E.

8.
throw away
keep
Cut

9.
Turn to put
point F at top.
Cut a "door" in
the "tepee."

10.
Cut out pieces along
all four sides.

11.
Unfold.

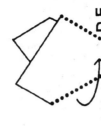

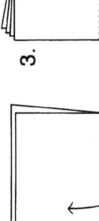
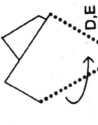

FS-32049 Science

Name _____

Hail, Sleet and Glaze

Hail looks like marbles made of ice. They can be bigger than baseballs! A hailstone starts as a raindrop in a thundercloud. It freezes and falls within the big cloud. Then it is lifted by wind to freeze and fall again. Each time it grows bigger. When it is too heavy to be lifted again, it falls to the ground. Hailstorms happen in the summer.

Sleet is smaller than hail. It begins to fall as rain. When it passes through a cold layer of air, it freezes. It lands as a bead of ice. Sleet falls in the winter.

Sometimes the air is warm but the ground is freezing. Then when it rains, the water freezes as it hits the ground. This coating of ice is called glaze.

Let's Make a Book!

Look in books for pictures of thunderclouds. Read more about these summer storms. Draw a picture of a hailstorm for your book.

Write the answers to the questions.

1. Where do hailstones freeze? _____

_____

2. When do hailstorms happen? _____

_____

3. When does sleet freeze? _____

_____

4. When do you see sleet? _____

_____

Name

Wind

When air changes from hot to cold or cold to hot, it moves. This moving of air is called <u>wind</u>.

If the wind comes from the north, it is a north wind. If it comes from the west, it is a west wind.

Wind has a lot to do with weather. South winds usually bring warm weather. North winds bring cold. East winds may bring clouds and west winds, blue skies.

Miles Per Hour	Kinds of Wind
1-3	Calm
4-31	Breeze
32-63	Gale
64-75	Storm
over 75	Hurricane

Write the answers to the questions.

1. What causes wind? _____

_____

2. Wind from the east is an _____ wind.

3. What two winds may bring nice weather? _____

_____

4. What two winds may bring poor weather? _____

_____

NORTH

Let's Make a Book!

You can make your own wind—by blowing! And it is strong enough to move something— like a pinwheel.

Fold a 6″ square of paper crossways as shown: Now cut along these fold lines from each corner <u>almost</u> to the center.

Bend A, B, C and D corners to center. Push a pin through and into pencil eraser.

BLOW!

33

Name _____

Storms

Some storms bring rain. Some bring snow. But all storms bring terrific winds!

Hurricanes are strong storms. They can reach a speed of almost 200 miles per hour. They travel westward over the Atlantic Ocean. When they strike land, they can do a lot of damage.

Typhoons are like hurricanes, but they are Pacific Ocean storms.

A tornado is also called a twister. It has a long funnel that sucks up houses and cars like a giant vacuum cleaner! This wind can blow more than 300 miles per hour. It is the fastest wind.

Another name for any of these storms is <u>cyclone.</u>

Write the answers to the questions.

1. All storms bring _____ .

2. What ocean do hurricanes travel over? _____

3. Where do you find a typhoon? _____

4. What is the fastest wind? _____

5. Any of these storms could also be called a _____ .

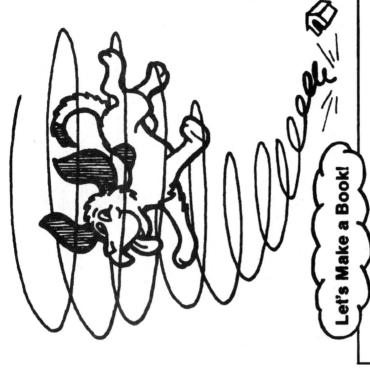

Let's Make a Book!

Choose a story starter to write an adventure story:

1. All morning they've been saying that a hurricane was on its way. My neighbors are leaving to find a safe place to wait. But I can't leave because . . .

2. I lived in a small town in Texas. We raised cotton. Last week something awful happened: a tornado hit! It began on Tuesday. We were all watching those clouds . . .

34

Name _____

Thunder and Lightning

A thundercloud is HUGE! It can start one mile above ground and go up 11 miles!

The thundercloud is heavy with water drops. Sometimes the drops get very big. Strong winds blow them apart! When this happens, it makes two clouds. It also makes sparks of electricity. Lightning is electricity. Sometimes it shoots from one cloud to the ground.

When lightning flashes, it quickly heats up the air. This makes the air move. Hot air charges one way. Cold air blasts another way. This crashing of air together in the sky is thunder.

The light and sound of a thunderstorm have to travel to our eyes and ears. Light travels faster than sound. So we see the lightning before we hear the thunder.

Let's Make a Book!

Make a cut-and-paste picture of a thunderstorm. Look at books to get ideas. Put a 12" x 18" blue paper the tall way. Cut a giant gray cloud. You'll need yellow for lightning. Add anything else you wish.

Write the answers to the questions.

1. How tall can a thundercloud be? _____

2. What makes lightning? _____
_____

3. Lightning is _____
_____

4. What is thunder? _____
_____

35   FS-32049 Science

Name

Skill: Finding Information

Dew and Frost

Some mornings you may look outside to a bright blue sky. But all the ground is wet. "Did it rain?" you wonder. No, it is <u>dew</u>. Dew does not fall from clouds as rain. But it does come out of the air.

Air is full of water vapor. You cannot see it. At night the ground cools off. The bits of vapor come close to the cool grass. They get cool. They stick to the grass. They condense to drops of water.

<u>Frost</u> happens in the same way. If the ground is freezing cold, the vapor turns to ice. Everything looks white, as if snow has fallen.

You find dew and frost when the sky is clear. Clouds act like a blanket. They keep the earth too warm for dew and frost to form.

Write the answers to the questions.

1. What wetness does not fall from clouds? —————

2. Where did the dew come from? —————

3. What happens when the vapor comes near something cold? —————

4. What looks white like snow? —————

5. When do you find dew and frost? —————

Let's Make a Book!

It's time to put your book together! Make a nice cover, showing some kind of weather. Get your pages in order. Staple. Now, pass the books around the room so you can read each others'!

FS-32049 Science

What's in Our Solar System?

An *astronomer*, or scientist who studies the universe, might make this list if you asked her what is in our solar system.

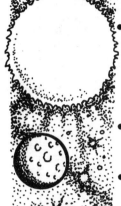

- one **star**, or hot glowing ball of gases, called the Sun

- all the planets' moons

- small chunks of rock or ice called **meteoroids**

- lots of empty space

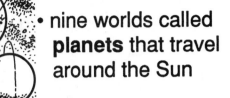

- nine worlds called **planets** that travel around the Sun

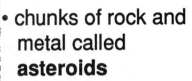

- chunks of rock and metal called **asteroids**

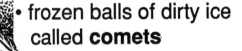

- frozen balls of dirty ice called **comets**

Write a definition for each of these words.

1. astronomer _____

_____

2. star _____

3. planets _____

_____

4. asteroids _____

5. meteoroids _____

_____

6. comets _____

_____

Brainwork! Find *solar system* in a dictionary or in the glossary of a science book. Write the definition you find.

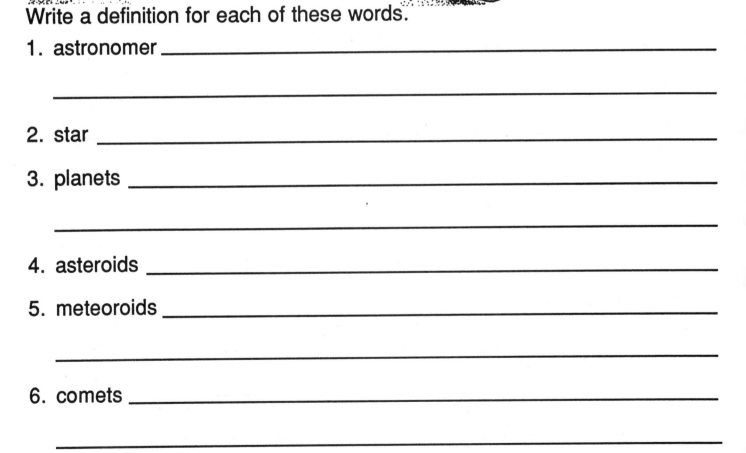

Our Sun

When you see the Sun shining during the day, you are seeing a star. A star is a huge glowing ball of gases. The Sun is the only star in our solar system. It looks much larger than the stars we see at night because it is closer to us than the others. Even so, the Sun is 93 million miles from Earth.

Our Sun is really only a medium-size star. Some other stars in the universe are much bigger, and many stars are much smaller. The Sun is a yellow star. Hotter stars are blue and cooler stars are red.

Copy the sentence from the story that answers each question.

1. What is a star? _____

_____

2. Which star is in our solar system? _____

_____

3. How far is the Sun from Earth? _____

_____

4. What color is the Sun? _____

5. Why does the Sun look larger to us than other stars?

_____

_____

_____

Brainwork! The Sun's light and heat help Earth's plants and animals to grow. Draw a picture to show this.

The Planets Are Moving!

Each of the planets in our solar system **revolves**, or travels, around the Sun. The planets circle the Sun along paths called **orbits**. Because the planets are at different distances from the Sun, each one takes a different length of time to revolve once.

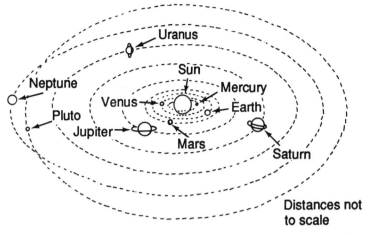

Distances not to scale

1. What word means *travels around*? _____

2. What are the planets' paths around the sun called? _____

3. Why do the planets take different lengths of time to revolve around the

   Sun?_____

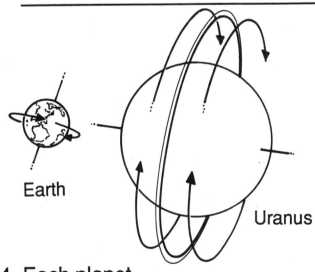

Earth

Uranus

Each planet in our solar system **rotates**, or **spins**, around a line through its center. This imaginary line is called an **axis**. It takes each planet a different length of time to rotate once.

4. Each planet _____ around a line through its center.

5. This imaginary line is called an _____.

6. *Rotates* means _____.

Brainwork! Use two things from your desk. Move one so it revolves around the other. Then put one down and move the other so it rotates.

 FS-32049 Science

Solar System Scramble

Unscramble the name of each numbered object below. Write the name on the correct line below.

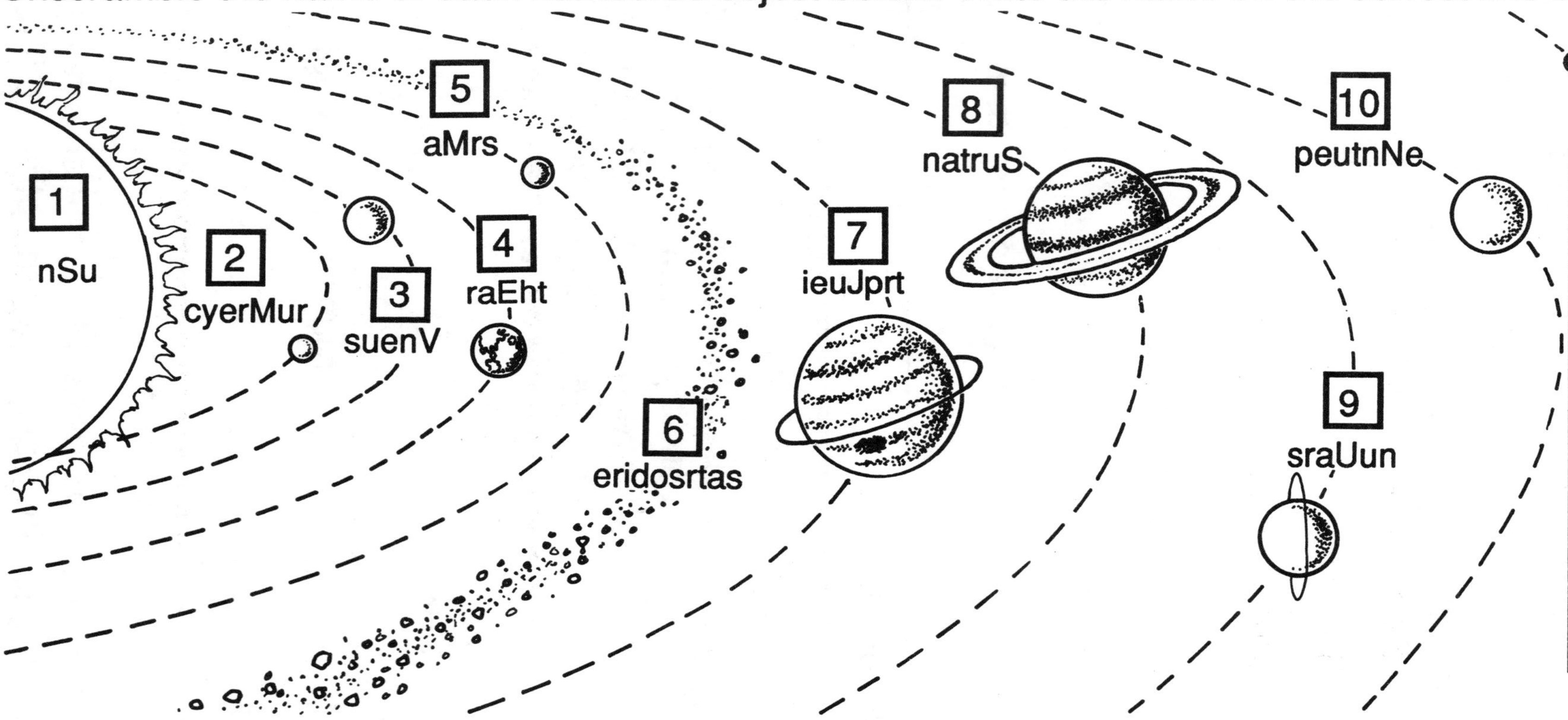

Word Box
Neptune
asteroids
Mars
Earth
Jupiter
Sun
Saturn
Uranus
Pluto
Venus
Mercury

11 tuloP

10 peutnNe

9 sraUun

8 natruS

7 ieuJprt

6 eridosrtas

5 aMrs

4 raEht

3 suenV

2 cyerMur

1 nSu

1. _____

2. _____

3. _____

4. _____

5. _____

6. _____

7. _____

8. _____

9. _____

10. _____

11. _____

Brainwork! Turn this paper over and write the names of the nine planets in our solar system.

A Strip of Space

Follow these directions to compare the positions of the planets from the Sun.

1. Color:

- the Sun yellow
- Mercury brown
- Venus yellow

- Earth green
- Mars red
- Jupiter orange

- Saturn yellow
- Uranus and Neptune blue
- Pluto purple

2. Cut out the four strips.

3. Glue:

- strip 2 to the right end of strip 1
- strip 3 to the right end of strip 2
- strip 4 to the right end of strip 3

(Distances are to approximate scale.)

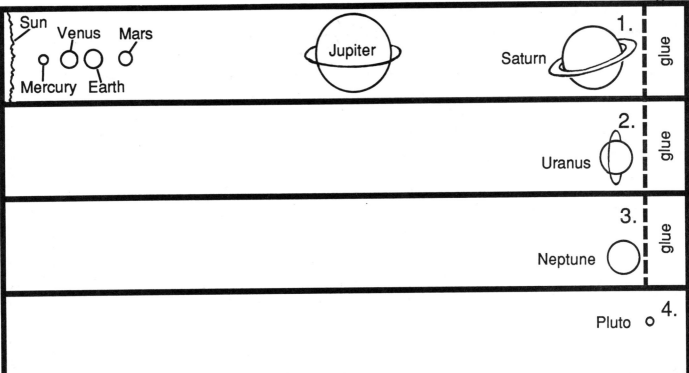

FS-32049 Science

Mercury—Closest to the Sun

Mercury is the planet closest to the Sun. That is why Mercury travels around the Sun faster than any other planet. It takes Mercury 88 days to revolve once around the Sun.

Little was known about Mercury before 1974. Scientists have a hard time studying Mercury with telescopes because of the Sun's great light. In 1974 and 1975 an unmanned spacecraft named *Mariner X* flew by Mercury three times and sent scientists new information about the planet.

The surface of Mercury is much like the moon's surface. It has high cliffs and deep craters, or holes. Mercury has almost no atmosphere, or gases surrounding it. Temperatures on the planet range from 950° F to –210° F! Mercury has no moons.

Write each answer in a sentence.

1. Which planet is closest to the Sun? _____

_____

2. How long does it take Mercury to revolve around the Sun? _____

_____

3. Why do scientists have a hard time studying Mercury with telescopes?

_____

4. What did Mariner X do? _____

_____

_____

5. Describe Mercury's surface. _____

_____

Brainwork! Make a list of three interesting facts about Mercury.

Venus—Earth's Twin

Use the words in the Word Bank to complete the story.

Word Bank			
light	against	lightning	size
closest	higher	atmosphere	melt

Venus has been called Earth's twin because it is about

the same _____ as Earth. Venus is the second
1

planet from the Sun and is the planet _____ to
2

Earth. Venus was also the first planet to be studied

by spacecraft. Venus has no moon.

Venus has an interesting _____ , or blanket
3

of gases around it. It reflects, or bounces off, so much of the Sun's

_____ that Venus is easier to see than any other planet. The
4

atmosphere also lets some sunlight in and traps heat _____ the
5

planet's surface. Therefore, temperatures on Venus are high enough to

_____ some metals. Clouds move at high speeds in Venus's
6

atmosphere, and bolts of _____ streak across its sky.
7

Venus has volcanoes on its surface and a mountain _____
8

than the highest on Earth. There is no liquid water on Venus. Earth's

plants and animals could not live on Venus.

Brainwork! Think of another nickname for Venus. Write to tell why it is a
good nickname.

Our Home Planet

Use the words from the Word Bank to complete the story.

Word Bank

closer   soil   Sun

distance   reaches   main   planet   Earth   liquid

The third planet from the _____ is our home planet Earth. Earth has

something no other _____ is known to have—living things.
2

Earth is at the right _____ from the Sun to have the liquid water
3

necessary to support life. Mercury and Venus are too hot because they are

_____ to the Sun. The other planets are too far from the Sun to
4

have _____ water. Not much heat or light _____ them, so the
5   6

water would be in the form of ice.

Earth has a lot of water. Most living things need water. Water helps to

control the earth's weather and climate. Water also breaks rocks into

_____ which plants need to grow.
7

Earth is surrounded by a blanket of air called the atmosphere. Oxygen is

one of the _____ gases in the atmosphere. Most animals breathe
8

oxygen.

_____ is a special planet!
9

Brainwork! Design a poster showing why Earth is a good planet for
living things.

We See Our Moon

Earth has one moon. It is the moon that we see in the sky. The moon is Earth's partner in space. It makes a path around, or **orbits**, Earth. It also orbits the Sun along with the earth.

The moon looks large because it is closer to Earth than the Sun or planets. Four moons would stretch across the **diameter**, or widest part of the earth.

In 1969 **astronaut** Neil Armstrong took the first steps on the moon. Scientists have studied rocks brought back from the moon.

The surface of the moon has many deep holes called **craters**. It has flat areas called **maria**. The moon also has rocky mountain areas called **highlands**. There is no air, wind, or water on the moon. No life exists there.

Write the word in dark print from the story that matches each definition.

1. deep holes in the moon's surface

2. to make a path around

3. flat land on the moon

_____   _____   _____

4. the widest part of the earth

5. areas with rocky mountains

6. a person who travels in space

_____   _____   _____

Write two sentences about the moon using two of the words in dark print.

1. _____

_____

2. _____

_____

Brainwork! Would you like to visit the moon? Write to explain your answer.

Mars—The Red Planet

Mars, the fourth planet from the Sun, is half the size of Earth. Mars has two moons. It has been called the Red Planet because of its red color. Parts of this planet's surface are covered with sand dunes and dry reddish deserts. Other areas look like dried up riverbeds. Some scientists believe water may once have flowed on Mars. Mars also has two polar caps made up of frozen water and dry ice. Pink, blue, and white clouds move through the Red Planet's sky.

For a long time some people thought there might be life on Mars. When two U.S. spacecraft landed on the planet in 1976, they sent back photographs of Mars and did experiments to find out if life exists there. Scientists now believe that Mars does not have plant or animal life like that on Earth.

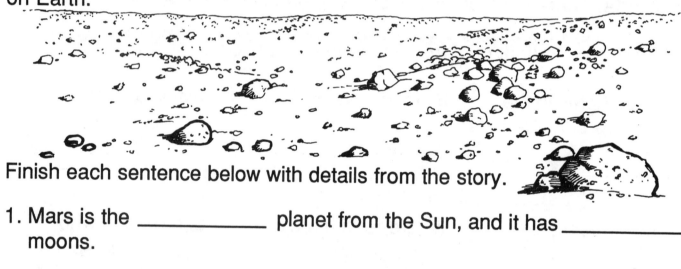

Finish each sentence below with details from the story.

1. Mars is the _____ planet from the Sun, and it has _____ moons.

2. Mars is nicknamed the _____.

3. Two U.S. spacecraft landed on Mars in _____ , sent back photographs, and did _____.

4. Mars has dry reddish _____ and what look like dried up _____.

5. Mars has two _____ made of frozen water and dry ice.

Brainwork! Draw and color a picture that shows your idea of the Red Planet's landscape.

Jumbo Jupiter

Jupiter is the largest of the nine planets. It is more than 11 times larger than Earth.

Jupiter is the fifth planet from the Sun, and it travels once around the Sun every 12 years. This jumbo planet rotates in just ten hours—faster than any other planet!

Thick clouds surround Jupiter. Most scientists believe that the belts of color in Jupiter's atmosphere are caused by different gases. The planet is a giant ball of liquids and gases with, perhaps, a small rocky core. Its famous Great Red Spot is a huge storm of swirling gases. Lightning streaks across Jupiter's sky. Jupiter has a thin dust ring around its middle and 16 known moons.

Jupiter's Great Red Spot

Write **true** or **false**.

_____ 1. Jupiter is the smallest planet in our solar system.

_____ 2. Earth is larger than Jupiter.

_____ 3. It takes 12 years for Jupiter to travel around the Sun.

_____ 4. Jupiter rotates faster than any other planet.

_____ 5. Jupiter's Great Red Spot is a huge storm of swirling gases.

_____ 6. Jupiter has a thick ice ring around its middle.

_____ 7. Jupiter has more than ten moons.

_____ 8. Jupiter is the sixth planet from the sun.

Brainwork! Write one true and one false statement about Jupiter. Have a friend tell which is true and which is false.

Stunning Saturn

Saturn is the sixth planet from the Sun. Saturn is best known for the beautiful rings around its middle. The rings are thin and flat and made of pieces of rock and ice. They stretch more than 100,000 miles across!

Some scientists believe the rings are made of particles left over from the time when Saturn first became a planet. Others believe the rings are made of pieces of a moon that was torn apart when it came too close to Saturn.

Saturn is the second largest planet. Since Saturn is more than nine times farther than Earth is from the Sun, it is much colder than Earth. The planet is a giant ball of spinning gases. Saturn has at least 20 moons.

Write each answer in a sentence.

1. For what is Saturn best known? _____

_____

2. What is one idea scientists have about how Saturn's rings were made?

_____

_____

3. How does Saturn compare in size with the other planets? _____

_____

4. Why is Saturn colder than Earth? _____

_____

5. How many moons does Saturn have? _____

_____

Brainwork! Write a poem about Saturn's beautiful rings.

The Blue-green Giants

Uranus and Neptune are giant planets more than a billion miles from the Sun and Earth. They are about the same size. Each is more than $3\frac{1}{2}$ times larger than Earth. They look blue-green in photos because both have a gas called methane in their atmospheres. Uranus and Neptune are very cold planets where life probably doesn't exist.

Uranus is the seventh planet from the Sun. It is known to have at least 15 moons and 11 thin rings. Uranus rotates in the direction opposite to that of Earth. It can be seen from Earth without a telescope.

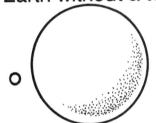

Neptune is farther from the Sun than Uranus. It has eight known moons. Some astronomers believe it may also have a ring. Neptune cannot be seen without a telescope.

Decide which planet or planets each fact describes. If it describes Uranus, write *Uranus*. If it describes Neptune, write *Neptune*. If it describes both Uranus and Neptune, write *both*.

1. rotates in the opposite direction

_____

2. called a blue-green giant

_____

3. cannot be seen without a telescope

_____

4. is more than a billion miles from Earth

_____

5. has methane in its atmosphere

_____

6. has at least 11 rings

_____

7. can be seen without a telescope

_____

8. has eight known moons

_____

Brainwork! List three ways Uranus and Neptune are alike. List three ways they are different.

Faraway Pluto

Pluto travels farther from the Sun than any other planet in our solar system. At its farthest point, it is more than four billion miles from Earth!

Pluto is also the smallest of the nine known planets. It is smaller than Earth's moon.

Scientists know very little about the planet Pluto because it is so far away. It is believed to be like a rocky snowball in space. Charon is Pluto's only moon. Scientists don't think any life exists on faraway Pluto.

Earth

Pluto

Greatest distance: 4,670,000,000 miles

Unscramble each sentence so it tells one fact about Pluto. Write the fact.

1. farthest Sun Pluto travels from the

_____

2. has moon one Pluto

_____

3. planet smallest Pluto is the

_____

4. travels billion more four than Earth from miles Pluto

_____

_____

5. Pluto's named is Charon moon

_____

Brainwork! Write two questions you would like to ask an astronomer about Pluto or its moon.

FS-32049 Science

So Far Apart

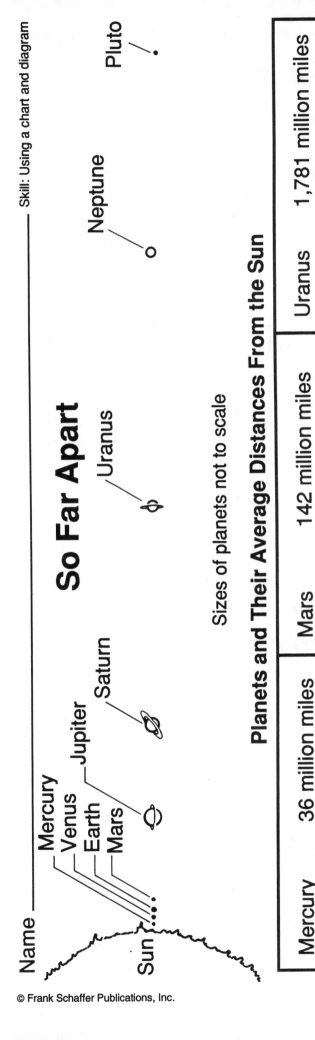

Sizes of planets not to scale

Planets and Their Average Distances From the Sun

Mercury	36 million miles	Mars	142 million miles	Uranus	1,781 million miles
Venus	67 million miles	Jupiter	484 million miles	Neptune	2,788 million miles
Earth	93 million miles	Saturn	885 million miles	Pluto	3,660 million miles

Use the chart and diagram to answer these questions.

1. What is Neptune's average distance from the Sun?
   _____

2. Which planet has an average distance from the Sun of 142 million miles?
   _____

3. Which planet is closest to the Sun—Saturn, Mars, or Neptune?
   _____

4. How much farther from the Sun is Venus than Mercury?
   _____

5. How much farther is the fourth planet from the Sun than the third planet from the Sun?
   _____

Brainwork! Write why you think it is difficult for people to travel to other planets.

The Planets' Names

Match each symbol in the puzzle to a clue below. Write the planet's name across or down in capital letters.

Across

ψ Neptune was named after the Roman god of the sea.

♀ Venus was named after the Roman goddess of love and beauty.

♂ Mars was named after the Roman god of war.

♅ Uranus was named after the Greek god of the sky.

♇ Pluto was named after the Greek and Roman god of the lower world.

Down

☿ Mercury was named after the Roman messenger of the gods.

♃ Jupiter was named after the Roman king of the gods and ruler of the universe.

♄ Saturn was named after the Roman god of farming.

⊕ Earth was named after the Greek earth goddess.

Brainwork! Make a word search puzzle with the planets' names. Have a friend solve your puzzle.

FS-32049 Science

Name _____

My Planet Report

Name of the planet _____

Named after _____

Size of the planet _____

Average distance from the Sun _____

Time needed to revolve around the Sun _____

Time needed to rotate on its axis _____

Facts about the planet's surface _____

_____

Facts about the planet's moon(s) _____

_____

Other interesting facts _____

_____

My information came from

_____

_____

A picture of my planet

My planet's symbol

     FS-32049 Science

Interesting Moons

Use the code to discover the names of some moons in our solar system.

A	B	C	D	E	F	G	H	I	J	K	L	M
1	2	3	4	5	6	7	8	9	10	11	12	13

N	O	P	Q	R	S	T	U	V	W	X	Y	Z
14	15	16	17	18	19	20	21	22	23	24	25	26

A. Jupiter's moon named ___ ___ has at least eight active volcanoes.
       9 15

B. ___ ___ ___ ___ ___ ___ travels around Mars in $7\frac{1}{2}$ hours. No other
  16 8 15 2 15 19
moon travels so fast.

C. Jupiter also has the largest moon in the solar system. It is named

___ ___ ___ ___ ___ ___ ___ ___.
 7 1 14 25 13 5 4 5

D. ___ ___ ___ ___ ___ is known to have a thick atmosphere. It is one of
 20 9 20 1 14
Saturn's moons.

E. Neptune's moon ___ ___ ___ ___ ___ ___ orbits the planet backwards.
               20 18 9 20 15 14

F. ___ ___ ___ ___ ___ ___ is the smallest Martian moon.
 4 5 9 13 15 19

G. ___ ___ ___ ___ ___ ___ is one of Jupiter's 16 moons.
 5 21 18 15 16 1

H. The first footsteps on another surface in space

were taken on Earth's ___ ___ ___ ___.
                  13 15 15 14

Brainwork! Which moon above would you most like to visit? Write a
paragraph telling which moon you would choose and why.

Name _____

Beyond Our Solar System

Astronomers know that much lies beyond our solar system. In fact, in the drawing on this page our solar system is just a tiny speck in a larger group of objects in space. This larger group is called the Milky Way galaxy. The Milky Way is made up of all the stars you can see in the night sky and many more beyond those. It also contains large clouds made of gas and dust. But that's not all! Beyond our Milky Way, astronomers have seen millions of other galaxies. Each of these has billions of stars. Astronomers call space and everything in it the universe.

Side View of the Milky Way

← Our Solar System

1. What is the name of our galaxy? _____

2. What have astronomers seen beyond our galaxy? _____

3. What is the universe? _____

4. Which contains the largest group of objects—the solar system, the universe, or the Milky Way? _____

5. What two kinds of objects does the Milky Way contain? _____

Brainwork! Write a mini-book about the universe. Use the words *planet, solar system,* and *galaxy.*

55

A Review Riddle

Find a word in the Word Bank that matches each clue below. Write the word on the blanks.

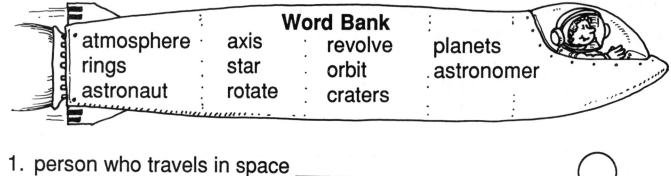

Word Bank

atmosphere · axis · revolve · planets
rings · star · orbit · astronomer
astronaut · rotate · craters

1. person who travels in space __ __ __ __ __ __ ◯ __ __

2. deep holes ◯ __ __ __ __ __ __

3. nine worlds __ ◯ __ __ __ __ __

4. to spin __ ◯ __ __ __ __ __

5. to travel around __ __ __ __ __ __ ◯ __

6. scientist who studies the objects in space

__ __ __ __ __ __ ◯ __ __ __ __ __

7. imaginary line through the center of a planet __ __ ◯ __

8. a planet's path around the sun ◯ __ __ __ __

9. ball of hot glowing gases __ __ ◯ __

10. Saturn, Jupiter and Uranus have these __ __ __ __ ◯

11. a blanket of gases __ __ __ __ __ __ __ ◯ __ __

Answer this riddle! Write the circled letters on the blanks below.

What is another name for our solar system?

__ __ __   __ __ __ __ __   __ __   __ __ __ __ __
8 1 4   11 3 9 2 5   7 6   10 11 9 2 5

Brainwork! Scramble the letters in each planet's name. Have a friend unscramble them.

FS-32049 Science

Sources of Heat

Find out about the many different ways we get heat. Look at these pictures. Then write a sentence about a source of heat by unscrambling each group of words. Remember to use capitals and periods!

Sun

Earth

1. earth   The   sun   the   heats

_____

_____

2. gives   heat   us   A   fire

_____

_____

3. hot   light   bulbs   makes   Electricity

_____

_____

4. heat   Gas   oil   and   homes

_____

_____

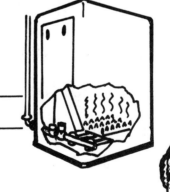

5. two   together   heat   Rubbing   things   makes

_____

_____

Try This! Heat is used for cooking. List three other uses for heat.

Fuels

Anything that is burned to produce heat is a fuel. People use fuels to heat homes, cook foods, and make hot water. Fuel also provides power for cars, trains, airplanes, and other kinds of transportation.

Long ago, people burned wood as fuel to make fire for heat and light. Later, people used oils from animal fat and plants to burn in lamps. The discovery of coal helped factories produce great amounts of power to make products. Today, petroleum, an oily liquid, is used to power most kinds of transportation. The natural gas that comes from wells drilled deep in the earth heats many homes.

USERS OF FUELS

Complete the sentences by filling in the missing letters.

1. __ue__ is anything that is burned to produce heat.

2. Wood and oi__ are fuels.

3. Long ago, people used wood to make __ir__ .

4. People use fuels to __ea__ homes and __oo__ foods.

5. __oa__ is used in many factories.

6. __e__ __o__eu__ is used to power cars, trains, and airplanes.

7. Many homes are heated by __a__u__a__ __a__ .

Try This! Electricity is a type of fuel used to heat such things as stoves and dryers. List three things in your home that need electricity to produce heat.

Fahrenheit or Celsius?

A thermometer measures temperature.
Read about two kinds of scales used on thermometers.

Fahrenheit

The Fahrenheit scale is named after Gabriel Fahrenheit, a German scientist. On this scale, the freezing point of water is 32 degrees (32°F). This means that water turns from liquid to solid at 32°F. The boiling point of water is 212°F. A person's normal body temperature is 98.6°F. Most people in the United States use the Fahrenheit scale.

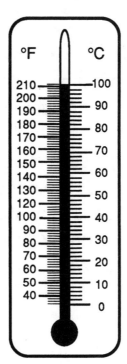

Celsius

The Celsius scale is named after Anders Celsius, a Swedish scientist. It is part of the metric system. Using this scale, the freezing point of water is 0 degrees (0°C) and the boiling point of water is 100°C. A person's normal body temperature is 37°C. Most countries around the world use the Celsius scale.

Read each phrase below. Write the name of the scale it describes.

1. water freezes at 0°

_____

2. part of the metric system

_____

3. water boils at 212°

_____

4. named after a German scientist

_____

5. used in most countries

_____

6. water freezes at 32°

_____

7. named after a Swedish scientist

_____

8. normal body temperature is 98.6°

_____

Try This! Do you think everyone in the world should use the same scale for measuring temperature? Write to explain your answer.

FS-32049 Science

Heat Travels

Heat travels from a warmer object to a cooler one. If you touch an ice cube, the heat moves from your finger to the ice. If you leave your finger on the ice, the ice cube will begin to melt. Suppose you touch a hot cup of tea. The heat from the cup will go to your fingers. OUCH! The heat from a hot pan will go to your hands and burn them if you don't use potholders to pick it up.

The movement of heat through solid materials is called **conduction**. Some materials are better conductors than others. That means they allow heat to pass through more quickly and easily. Aluminum and copper are good conductors. Wood and plastic are poor conductors.

Write the answers.

1. Does heat travel from a cold object to a hot one or from a hot object to a cold one? _____

_____

2. What happens to an ice cube when you touch it with your finger?

_____

3. Why should you use potholders to pick up a hot pan?_____

_____

4. What is the movement of heat through solid materials called?

_____

5. Name two good conductors. _____

6. Name two poor conductors. _____

Try This! Design a poster to remind your family to use potholders when touching hot things. Display the poster in your kitchen.

Finding Out About Heat

Use this index to write the correct page numbers on the blanks below.

Celsius, Anders, 53

Coal, how it is formed, 20–21

Fahrenheit, Gabriel, 52–53

Fire, 12–19

Fuels, 20–26

Heat, sources of, 8–20;

how it travels, 38–40;

experiments, 60–61

Natural gas, 25–26

Petroleum, where it is found, 22;

petroleum products, 24–26

Sun, facts about, 8–11;

protection from, 43–44

Thermometers, kinds of, 52–53;

uses of, 54–55

Wood, 35–38

1. Heat experiments are discussed on pages _____.

2. Information on natural gas is on pages _____.

3. Pages _____ tell how heat travels.

4. Hints about protecting yourself from sunburn are on

pages _____.

5. Information about Gabriel Fahrenheit is on

pages _____.

6. The last page on which you will find something

about fire is page _____.

7. Facts about kinds of thermometers are on pages _____.

8. To find out the sun's temperature, look at pages _____.

9. You will find out about Anders Celsius on page _____.

10. Facts about wood are found on pages _____.

Try This! Design a cover for a book in which this index might be found.

Can You Take the Heat?

Use the words in the puzzle to answer the questions. Then color each space in the puzzle with the color given beside the question.

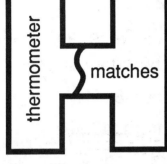
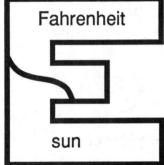
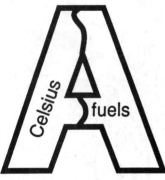
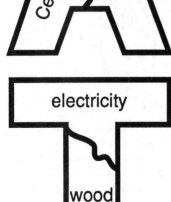

1. What star heats the earth? (yellow)

_____

2. What are coal and oil called? (green)

_____

3. What device measures temperature? (red)

_____

4. People long ago cut and burned this for heat and light. (orange)

_____

5. On this scale, the boiling point of water is 100 degrees. (green)

_____

6. Children should never play with these. (red)

_____

7. On this scale, the freezing point of water is 32 degrees. (yellow)

_____

8. This makes a toaster hot. (orange)

_____

Try This! Make a poster showing five ways to cool off on a hot day.

Sources of Light

Light can come from things found in nature. Most of our light comes from the sun. Light can also come from things made by people. For example, people make candles to use for light.

Some things that give light are pictured below. Decide whether they are found in nature or made by people. Write each one under the correct heading.

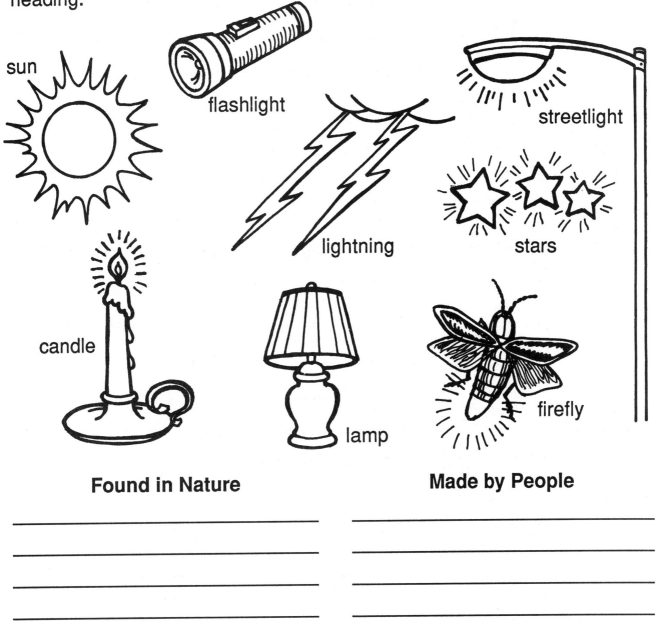

sun

flashlight

lightning

streetlight

stars

candle

lamp

firefly

Found in Nature

Made by People

_____   _____

_____   _____

_____   _____

_____   _____

Try This! Draw a picture of three things in your home that give off light.

Light and Sight

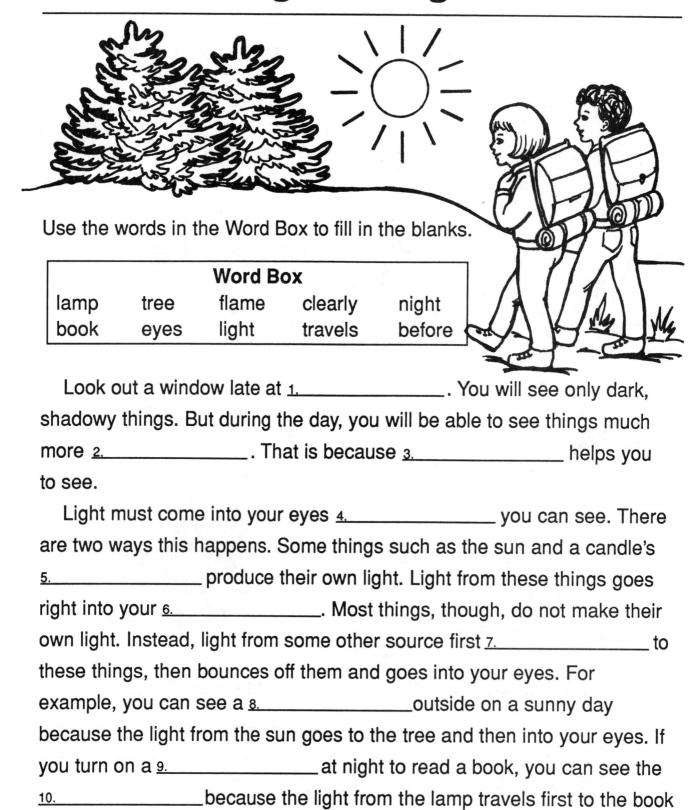

Use the words in the Word Box to fill in the blanks.

Word Box				
lamp	tree	flame	clearly	night
book	eyes	light	travels	before

Look out a window late at 1._____ . You will see only dark, shadowy things. But during the day, you will be able to see things much more 2._____ . That is because 3._____ helps you to see.

Light must come into your eyes 4._____ you can see. There are two ways this happens. Some things such as the sun and a candle's 5._____ produce their own light. Light from these things goes right into your 6._____ . Most things, though, do not make their own light. Instead, light from some other source first 7._____ to these things, then bounces off them and goes into your eyes. For example, you can see a 8._____ outside on a sunny day because the light from the sun goes to the tree and then into your eyes. If you turn on a 9._____ at night to read a book, you can see the 10._____ because the light from the lamp travels first to the book and then into your eyes.

Try This! What provides light in your classroom? Draw a picture of it.

Reflected Light

When light hits a mirror, it **bounces** off. It moves in a straight line and shines on another spot in the room. The **light** has been reflected.

Molly is standing in front of a **mirror**. Light is shining on her from a **lamp**. This light is reflected from her to the mirror. Then it is reflected to her eyes. Molly sees her **reflection** in the mirror.

Water, windows, and shiny **metal** also reflect light. Have you looked at the **moon** lately? It has no light of its own. Instead, light from the **sun** hits the moon and is reflected to the earth.

Use the **boldfaced** words in the story to complete the puzzle.

Across

2. The ___ has no light of its own.

4. When ___ hits a mirror, it is reflected.

6. Light from a ___ is shining on Molly.

7. We see our ___ in a mirror.

Down

1. The moon reflects light from the ___.

2. Shiny ___ reflects light.

3. Molly is looking in a ___.

5. Light ___ off a mirror.

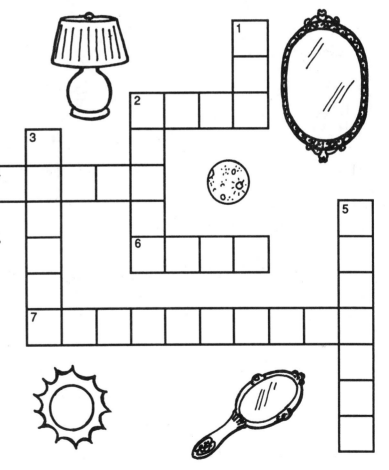

Try This! Explain how an automobile driver uses mirrors to drive safely.

FS-32049 Science

A Band of Colors

Did you know that sunlight is really made up of a band of different colors? You can see these colors with the help of a prism. A prism is a transparent piece of glass that usually has three sides. Hold the prism in front of a window and let the sun shine through it. Turn the prism so that the light appears on a wall. As the light passes through the glass, it is separated into red, orange, yellow, green, blue, indigo (deep violet-blue), and violet. These are the same colors that appear in a rainbow or in a spray of water from a garden hose. That is because drops of water act like prisms, separating sunlight into different colors as the light passes through them.

Color the band of colors.

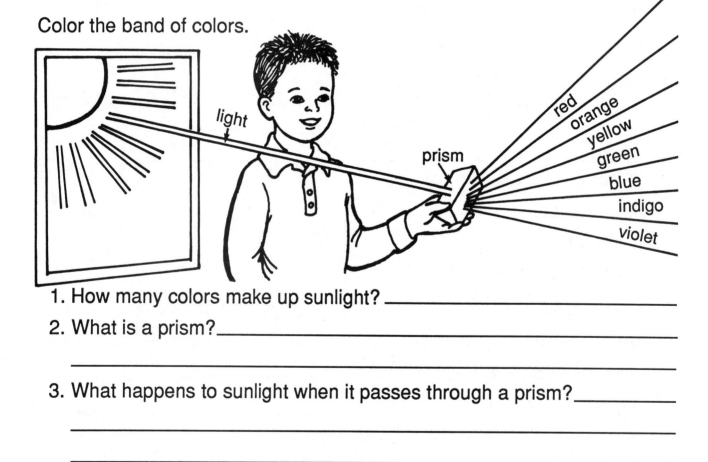

1. How many colors make up sunlight? _____

2. What is a prism? _____

_____

3. What happens to sunlight when it passes through a prism? _____

_____

_____

4. What happens when sunlight passes through a spray of water? _____

_____

_____

Try This! Design a bookmark that has all the colors of the rainbow.

The Speed of Light

Light travels about 186,000 miles a second. That is fast enough to go around the earth in the time it takes to blink an eye. It takes about eight minutes for light from the sun to reach the earth.

Scientists who study the stars are called **astronomers**. They call the distance light travels in one year a **light-year**. Light from a star named Alpha Centauri travels over four light-years to reach the earth. Light from Sirius, another star, travels eight and a half light-years to reach the earth!

Help each astronomer reach a star by following a path of words that form a sentence. Color the spaces as you go.

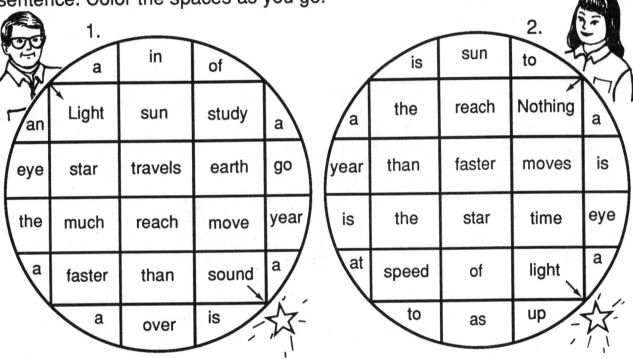

The sentences in the puzzle tell about the speed of light. Write them below. Don't forget capitals and periods!

1. _____

_____

2. _____

_____

Try This! Write a sentence about an astronomer's work. Scramble your sentence and have a friend unscramble it.

FS-32049 Science

A Listening Walk

The family in the picture is taking a "listening walk." On the lines below, match a word from **Box A** with one from **Box B** to write a phrase that describes each of the 12 different sounds they heard.

Box A		
bee	workers	water
bird	horn	jet
dog	baby	duck
bell	door	child

Box B		
honking	yelling	hammering
roaring	tweeting	splashing
barking	ringing	quacking
crying	buzzing	slamming

1. jet roaring

2. _____

3. _____

4. _____

5. _____

6. _____

7. _____

8. _____

9. _____

10. _____

11. _____

12. _____

Try This! Take a "listening walk." List 10 different sounds you hear.

FS-32049 Science

Animal Sounds

Below each picture, write the sound the animal makes. Use the words in the box.

roar	moo
meow	oink
baa	woof
croak	tweet
growl	buzz
cluck	chirp
quack	

cat

mosquito

1. _ _ _

2. _ _ _ _

sheep

cricket

3. _ _ _

4. _ _ _ _ _ _

dog

bear

pig

5. _ _ _ _

6. _ _ _ _ _

7. _ _ _ _

lion

duck

frog

8. _ _ _ _

9. _ _ _ _ _

10. _ _ _ _ _

chicken

cow

bird

11. _ _ _ _ _

12. _ _ _

13. _ _ _ _ _

Try This! List as many other animals and their sounds as you can in five minutes.

Noisy or Quiet?

Things that make loud, noticeable sounds are **noisy**. Things that make little or no sound are **quiet**. Cut out the pictures and paste them in the correct boxes.

FS-32049 Science

How We Hear

Read the paragraph to find out how we hear. Then cut apart the boxes on the right. Paste the sentences in the correct order on the left.

What happens when you hit a drum? You hear a sound, of course! But at that same instant many things are happening.

When the drum is hit, its top vibrates, or moves back and forth. The vibrations make sound waves that travel through the air. When the sound waves enter your ear, they hit your eardrum and make it vibrate. Nerves then carry the message to your brain and your brain tells you about the sound.

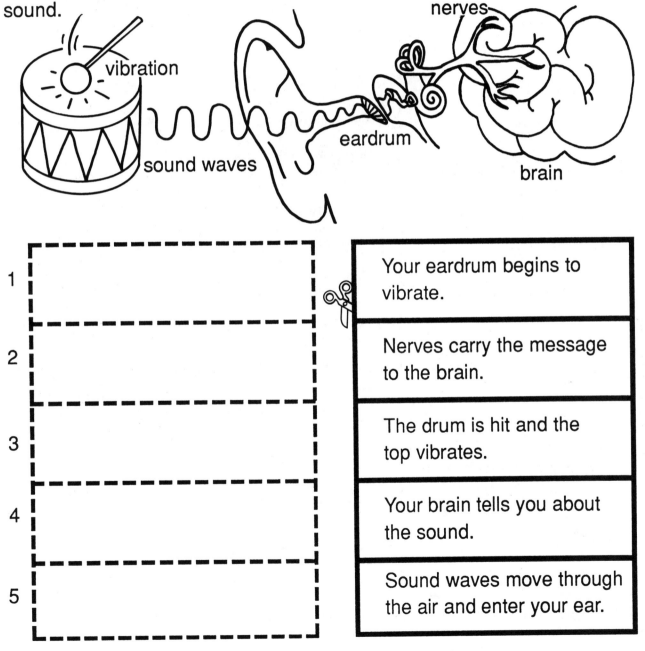

1

2

3

4

5

Your eardrum begins to vibrate.

Nerves carry the message to the brain.

The drum is hit and the top vibrates.

Your brain tells you about the sound.

Sound waves move through the air and enter your ear.

71

Hearing Vibrations

All sounds are made by **vibration**—the movement of an object back and forth. Short, small objects vibrate faster than long, large objects. The faster the vibration, the higher the sound.

Write the letters of the objects that make the highest sounds.

1. _____

2. _____

3. _____

4. _____

5. _____

6. _____

7. _____

Try This! Make a list of sounds that warn people of danger.

FS-32049 Science

Sound Travels

Mr. Hunter told his class these facts about sound.

> Sound waves are vibrations that move in all directions. They travel through gases (like air), liquids (like water), and solids (like glass). The closer you are to the source of the sound, the louder it seems.

The class did three experiments to learn how sound travels. On the lines write a conclusion they were able to draw from each experiment. Use the facts Mr. Hunter gave to help you.

1. Students stood in each corner of the classroom. Julio stood in the center and clapped his hands. All the students heard the clap at the same time.

_____

_____

2. The class stood on a sidewalk. The sound of a car became louder as it came closer. The sound became softer as the car got farther away from the students.

_____

_____

3. Jim put his ear against the side of an aquarium. Kate tapped two rocks together underwater. Jim heard the taps through the glass and the water.

_____

_____

Try This! Long ago, American Indians put their ears to the ground to find out if horsemen were approaching before any horses could be seen. Explain how they were able to do this.

Speak Up!

Put your fingers on your throat. Then read the next sentence out loud. You will feel the vocal cords inside your throat vibrating.

Down in the throat is the larynx, or voice box. To speak or sing, your brain sends messages telling the vocal cords to tighten. The air moving past the tightened cords causes them to vibrate. The vibrations make sounds. Working together, the tongue, shape of the lips, and vibration of the vocal cords let you make all the different sounds of the language you speak.

Write what each person below is saying. Use the sentences below.

I can feel my vocal cords vibrating in my throat.

My lips and tongue help me say my name—Lou!

My brain tells my vocal cords to tighten when I sing.

Two vocal cords stretch across the larynx.

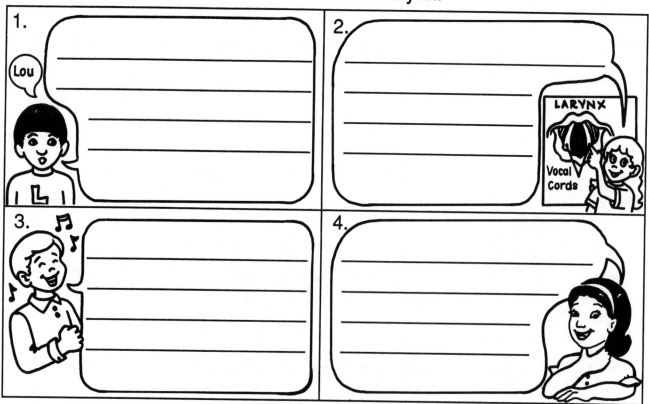

Try This! A ventriloquist talks without moving his lips. Make a bag puppet. Move the puppet's lips as you tell a joke like a ventriloquist.

Echoes

Jumping into a swimming pool makes waves. The waves bounce off the sides of the pool and come back to the swimmer. Sound waves do the same thing. When they hit something flat and hard they bounce back. Sound waves that bounce back are called **echoes**.

Tara heard an echo on the playground yesterday. When she shouted to Dan, the sound waves of her voice traveled through the air to him. Some of the sound waves hit the school wall and bounced back. These waves came back as an echo.

Tara stepped back from the wall and shouted to Dan again. She discovered that as she moved farther away from the wall, the sound waves took longer to travel to the wall and return to her as an echo.

Use the shape-blocks to fill in the missing words.

1. Water waves and ⬜⬜⬜⬜⬜ waves are alike because they both bounce back.

2. Sound waves bounce back when they hit something hard and ⬜⬜⬜⬜ .

3. Sound waves from Tara's ⬜⬜⬜⬜⬜ traveled through the air.

4. Some of the sound waves hit the school ⬜⬜⬜⬜ and bounced off.

5. Tara heard an ⬜⬜⬜⬜ after she shouted to Dan.

6. Tara stepped back and ⬜⬜⬜⬜⬜⬜ to Dan again.

7. The sound waves took longer to come back as Tara moved farther ⬜⬜⬜⬜ from the wall.

Try This! Bats send out high-pitched sounds as they fly at night. How do echoes warn them of danger and help them fly safely in the dark?

FS-32049 Science

A Sound Haiku Poem

Haiku poems are often about nature or the seasons. They have three lines containing a total of 17 syllables. The first line has 5 syllables, the second has 7 syllables, and the last has 5 syllables.

An example of a haiku poem:

On cold winter days
The wind howls and growls at me
From frosty white hills!

Use the lines below to create a haiku poem about the sounds heard in nature. Use your own descriptive words and some of the words below. Illustrate your poem in the box.

buzz
squish
ding
sizzle
plop
crackle
crash

splash
hoot
crunch
pop
zap
click

_____

_____

_____

_____

Try This! Create another haiku poem about your favorite kinds of musical sounds.

FS-32049 Science

What Makes Me Grow?

I am growing bigger every day. I can tell! I have a coat that used to fit me. Now it is too small. I know I am growing. And this is how it happens:

Every day my bones get bigger. My skin gets bigger. Every part of me gets bigger. That's because my body keeps making more of itself!

All of me—my blood, my brain, my lungs—is made of something very special, called cells. A cell is very, very small. I can't see them, but they are alive! There are billions of them inside of me, too!

1. What are you doing every day?

_____

2. How can you tell?

_____

_____

_____

3. How do you get bigger?

_____

_____

_____

4. My whole body is made of:

_____

5. Why can't I see the cells?

_____

6. How many are there?

_____

TRY THIS: Have someone mark your height on a wall at home. Every six months mark it again. Date it. We grow at different rates, so it may take years to see your growth. But it's fun to watch!

FS-32049 Science

Name _____ Date _____

Billions of Cells!

Cells have many shapes. Some are round like a ball. Some are round and flat like a coin. Some are two feet long! Some cells live only a few days. Some live all my life.

Cells can be different in some ways. But most are alike in important ways. They are made the same on the inside. They can make more of themselves. **A cell can divide itself to become two cells!**

There are billions and billions of cells in me. And just think— when my life began, I was only one cell big!

nerve cell

bone cells

1. What is one way cells can be different?

_____

_____

2. Name two ways most cells are alike.

_____

_____

_____

_____

red blood cells

3. How do cells make more of themselves?

_____

_____

4. How did you begin?

_____

muscle cells

TRY THIS: Look in the library for books about cells. How many shapes and kinds can you find? Draw some. Be sure to label them.

FS-32049 Science

What Gives Me My Shape?

Sometimes at Halloween we scare people with play skeletons. But we shouldn't be afraid of skeletons. A skeleton cannot do anything by itself. It can only move inside of you and me.

I have to have a skeleton! If I did not, I would be floppy like a jellyfish! My skeleton gives me my shape. It also protects the important soft parts inside of me.

My skeleton is made of over 200 bones. They are locked together, but can still move. My bones are made of cells. They are alive and growing bigger every day!

1. Why shouldn't you be afraid of a skeleton?

_____

_____

2. When can skeletons move?

_____

_____

3. About how many bones do you have?

_____

4. Why do we have skeletons?

_____

_____

_____

5. Why can your skeleton get bigger?

_____

_____

6. What would you be like without a skeleton?

_____

_____

TRY THIS: Feel to find your ribs, your backbone, your jaw. What other bones can you feel on your skeleton?

FS-32049 Science

Name _____ Date _____

I can name these bones on my skeleton!

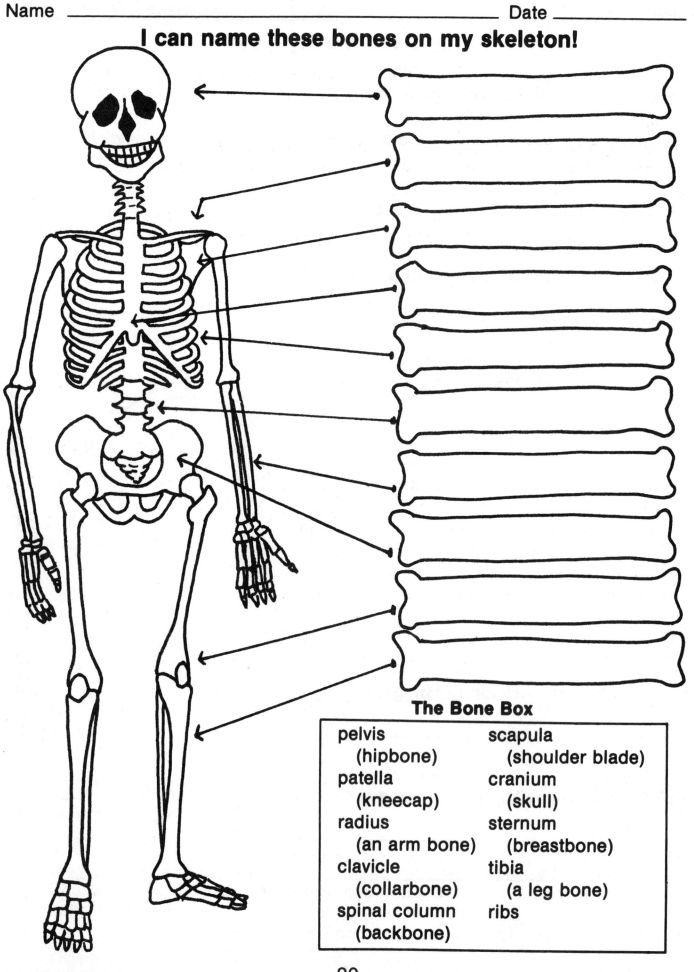

The Bone Box

pelvis
  (hipbone)
patella
  (kneecap)
radius
  (an arm bone)
clavicle
  (collarbone)
spinal column
  (backbone)

scapula
  (shoulder blade)
cranium
  (skull)
sternum
  (breastbone)
tibia
  (a leg bone)
ribs

FS-32049 Science

What Makes Me Move?

I have a skeleton to give me my shape. But what makes my skeleton move? My muscles do! Almost all of me is covered with muscles. Muscles move my body.

Muscles move my bones by pulling them. A muscle can pull because it can shorten itself. Muscles cannot push. It takes one pair of muscles to pull my arm up. It takes another pair to pull my arm down.

There are more than 500 muscles in my body. The more I use them, the stronger they get. That's why I should run and exercise a lot.

1. What moves your body?

_____

2. How do muscles work?

_____

_____

3. What can't muscles do?

_____

4. How many muscles are needed to raise and lower your arm?

_____

5. How many muscles do you have?

_____

6. Why is it important to get lots of exercise?

_____

WOW!

31

TRY THIS: Stand up. Hold your hand on one of your calves. Now raise up on your tiptoes. Go up and down two or three times. You will feel your muscles working!

FS-32049 Science

Name _____ Date _____

Why Do I Need to Eat?

My cells are alive, so they need food. All living things must eat. The food for my cells comes from what I eat. They cannot chew hamburgers and cake! They need the basic foods like sugar, fat, starch, and so on. All the food I eat is made of the basic foods.

My stomach breaks down the food I eat into a liquid. Then it becomes the basic food that cells need. My blood takes this basic food to my cells. The cells don't eat like I eat. They burn food. There is no flame, but it does make heat. That's why my body is warm. And that's what gives me energy!

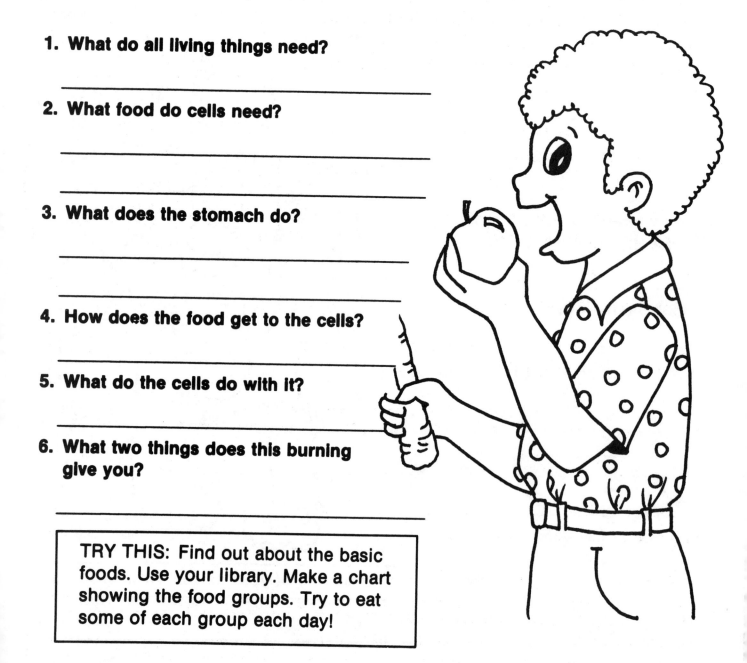

1. **What do all living things need?**

   _____

2. **What food do cells need?**

   _____

   _____

3. **What does the stomach do?**

   _____

   _____

4. **How does the food get to the cells?**

   _____

5. **What do the cells do with it?**

   _____

6. **What two things does this burning give you?**

   _____

TRY THIS: Find out about the basic foods. Use your library. Make a chart showing the food groups. Try to eat some of each group each day!

FS-32049 Science

How Does Eating Work?

I put food in my mouth and chew. My saliva (spit) mixes with it and I swallow. This "mush" goes down a tube to my stomach. My stomach muscles churn the food. They work on it for about four hours. The liver helps to break it down. It is almost like soup by then.

Now it goes through a gate of muscles into my small intestine. The food is worked on some more. At last it is broken down to the basic foods. It leaves the intestine through millions of tiny tubes. It goes into the blood. Waste is left behind and goes through the large intestine and out of my body.

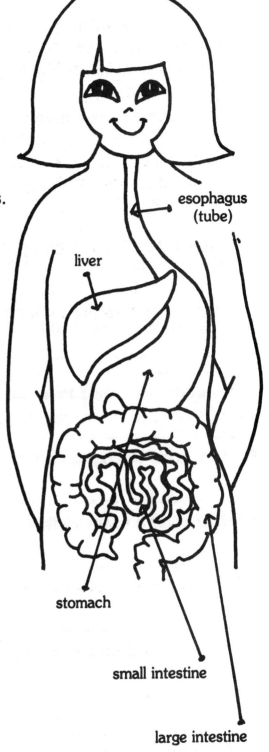

esophagus (tube)

liver

stomach

small intestine

large intestine

1. What is in your mouth to help you swallow?

_____

2. What churns the food?

_____

3. How long does it take?

_____

4. Where does it go next?

_____

5. How does the food get into the blood?

_____

_____

6. What is left behind?

_____

TRY THIS: Draw a diagram (picture) of the digestive (eating) part of you. Look in books. Label the parts. Learn the words.

FS-32049 Science

Name _____ Date _____

Why Do I Need to Breathe?

In the air is a gas called oxygen. Oxygen is needed when you build a fire. No burning can happen without oxygen.

For my body's cells to burn food, they need oxygen. That is why I must breathe!

I breathe in. I take in air. It goes to my lungs. My lungs take the oxygen out of the air. This goes into my blood. The blood takes it to my cells. Now my cells can burn or "eat" the food.

1. Name a gas that is in the air.

_____

2. What do you need for burning?

_____

3. What do cells need before they can "eat"?

_____

4. What do the lungs take out of the air?

_____

5. How does the oxygen get to the cells?

_____

6. Now what can the cells do?

_____

TRY THIS: Find out all you can about oxygen. Also, find out why green plants are so important to us!

FS-32049 Science

How Does Breathing Work?

I can breathe through my nose or my mouth. It's better to breathe through my nose, though. In my nose are many little hairs. It is also wet inside my nose. The air I breathe in is dirty. As it flows over these wet hairs, it becomes clean and warm. If there is too much dirt in the air, I sneeze or cough it out. The clean air then goes down my windpipe to my lungs.

My lungs are filled with millions of air sacs. They are like balloons. Air fills these sacs in my lungs. The oxygen in the air goes through them into the blood. The part of the air I don't need I breathe out.

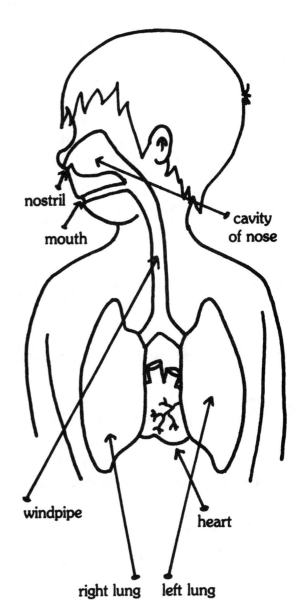

1. What cleans the air you breathe?

_____

2. What else happens to the air?

_____

3. Why do you sneeze?

_____

_____

4. What fills your lungs?

_____

5. What goes through the sacs and into the blood?

_____

6. What do you do with the air you don't need?

_____

TRY THIS: Draw a diagram of the breathing part of you. Label the parts. Learn the words.

Name _____ Date _____

Why Do I Need Blood?

My cells need food and oxygen. How do they get it? My blood takes it to them!

The blood leaves my heart. It carries food and oxygen. It travels through tubes called **arteries**. It delivers its load to the cells.

After burning a fire in the fireplace, what is left? Ash. After cells have burned food, there is a waste left too. It is a gas called **carbon dioxide**.

The blood picks up this gas. It travels now through veins. It goes back to the heart and lungs. The lungs take this waste gas and I breathe it out.

1. **What does the blood carry in the arteries?**

   _____

2. **What is left after cells burn food?**

   _____

3. **What does the blood pick up?**

   _____

4. **What does the blood flow through now?**

   _____

5. **Where does it go?**

   _____

6. **How do you get rid of the waste gas?**

   _____

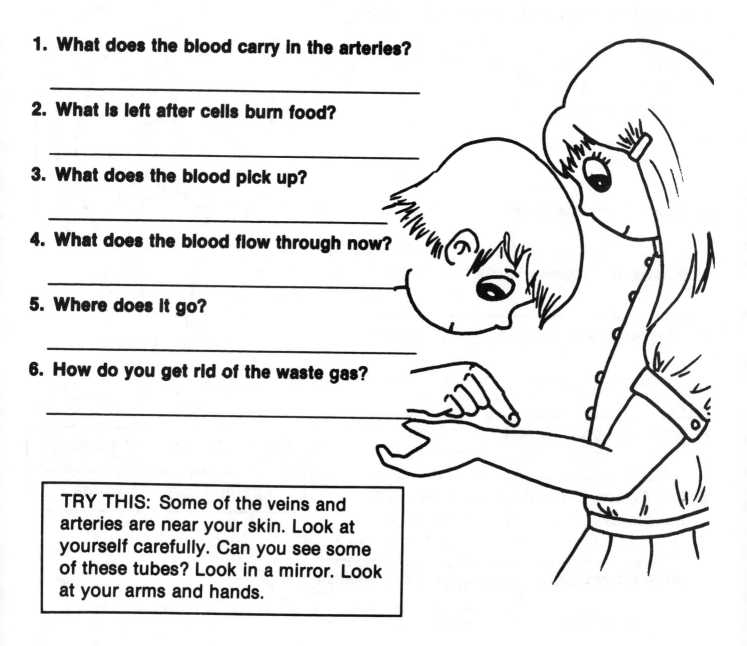

TRY THIS: Some of the veins and arteries are near your skin. Look at yourself carefully. Can you see some of these tubes? Look in a mirror. Look at your arms and hands.

FS-32049 Science

What Keeps My Blood Moving?

My blood moves because it is being pushed. It is pushed by a very strong pump: the heart.

My heart is not big. It is about the size of a fist. It weighs less than a pound. But it is strong! It is a bag of muscle. It has four "rooms." It has two pumps.

This powerful "machine" keeps nine pints of blood flowing. It flows through more than 60,000 miles of tubes! The blood goes all through the body. My heart is just terrific!

1. How does your heart move your blood?

_____

2. How big is your heart?

_____

3. How much does it weigh?

_____

4. Of what is it made?

_____

5. How many pints of blood are in the body?

_____

6. How many miles of tubes are there?

_____

TRY THIS: Press your hand on the side of your neck, up near your jawbone. Feel the beat of your heart. Run fast. Feel again. See how your heart beats faster now? It is pushing the blood faster to feed the cells faster. This gives you quick energy.

About Body Waste

It is like a busy city inside my body. A busy city contains garbage, dirty air and water. If things are not kept clean, people get sick.

It is the same in my body. If it did not get rid of the waste, I would get sick. So I breathe out the bad air. The solid waste goes out through my large intestine. But I still have to get rid of dirty water.

My blood carries this waste to my two kidneys. They take it out of my blood, and send it to my bladder. When my bladder is full, I send the waste out of my body. I lose over a quart of water a day!

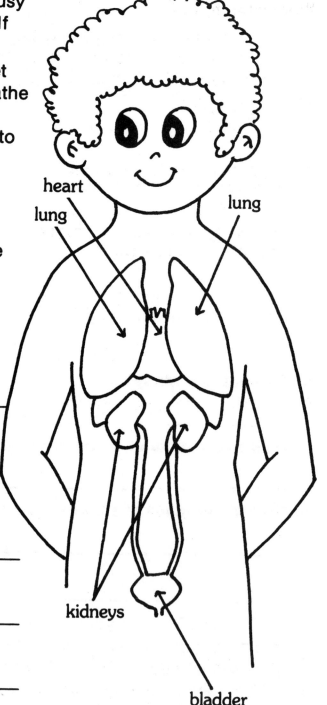

1. **What happens to the bad air in you?**

   _____

2. **What does the solid waste go through?**

   _____

3. **Where is the bad water taken out of the blood?**

   _____

4. **How many kidneys do you have?**

   _____

5. **Where does the bad water go?**

   _____

6. **How much water do you lose each day?**

   _____

FS-32049 Science

What Makes Everything Work?

The brain is the most wonderful computer in the world! I have a great body of moving parts. But none of these parts can act on their own. Something must tell them what to do!

My brain tells them. Here is what happens: if I want to sit down, my brain sends a message to the right muscles. The message is carried by my nerves. The brain says, "Pull," and they pull. It tells other muscles to relax, and they do. Then I am sitting!

My heart, lungs, stomach—all of me—works because of my brain!

1. What machine is the brain like?

_____

2. What tells your heart to beat?

_____

3. Why do your lungs breathe?

_____

_____

4. Why does the stomach work?

_____

_____

5. Who are the messengers?

_____

TRY THIS: Get a friend to play this game with you. Name something that your brain tells your body to do, like "Blink an eye," or "Wiggle my toes." Say it before your friend counts to five. then your friend gets a turn. How many can you name?

FS-32049 Science

How Do My Nerves Work?

My nerves are run by electricity! When the doorbell rings, the sound goes in my ears. An electrical charge goes along a path of my nerves to my brain. My brain tells me the doorbell is ringing. It sends the message to my muscles. They move me to the door.

I have billions of nerve cells. They start from all parts of my body. Most of them go up my spine. They go to the brain. Half of them send messages to my brain. The others take the message from the brain to the muscles and other parts of the body. Then they go into action.

1. What moves your nerve cells?

_____

2. Where does the message go?

_____

3. What do most of your nerves go through?

_____

4. How many nerve cells do you have?

_____

5. Where do they start?

_____

_____

6. Nerve cells take messages to my:

_____

_____

TRY THIS: Get a set of Dominos. Stand them up tall, about an inch apart in a long line. Tap the first one. It will fall on the second one. That one will fall on the third one, and so on. This is a little like the way a message travels through your nerves.

FS-32049 Science

What Else Does My Brain Do?

I am glad my brain keeps my body working. But if that is all it did, I would be just an animal!

My brain has three parts. The smallest part, at the bottom, is the **medulla**. This part keeps my body living. It keeps the heart beating and the lungs breathing.

The part above it is the **cerebellum**. This part moves my muscles. It's also where I keep my balance.

The biggest part is the **cortex**. Here is where I think and decide, I remember and enjoy, I feel and understand.

4 + 8 + 6 = hm-m-m-m!

1. What part of the brain keeps your body living?

_____

2. What part moves your muscles?

_____

3. Where does the thinking happen?

_____

4. What part keeps you breathing?

_____

5. What part keeps your balance?

_____

6. What makes you enjoy things?

_____

TRY THIS: Draw a diagram of the brain. Label the parts. Find out more about the cortex. Each kind of nerve reports to its part of the brain (example: seeing and hearing). Mark those places.

Name _____ Date _____

My Brain

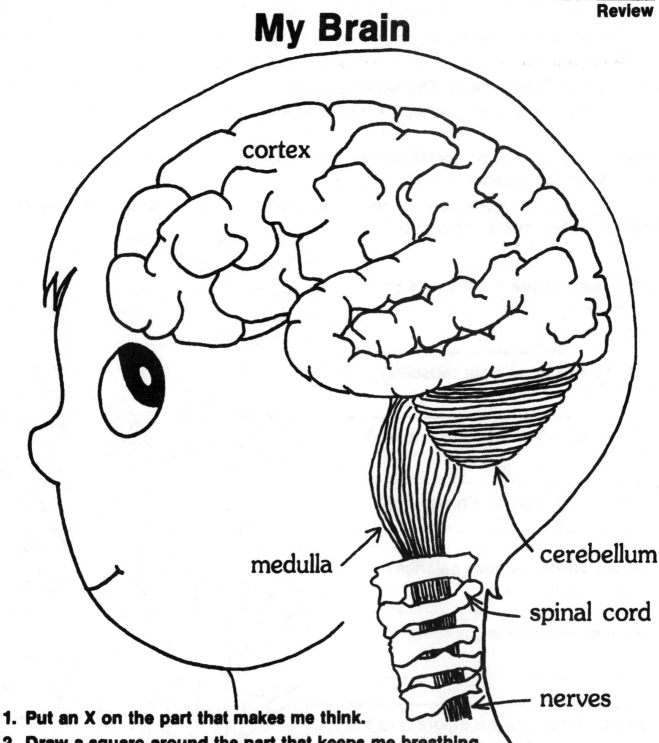

1. **Put an X on the part that makes me think.**
2. **Draw a square around the part that keeps me breathing.**
3. **Draw a circle around the part that moves my muscles.**
4. **Color the parts where most of the nerves go through.**
5. **In blue, color the parts that are "messengers."**

What About My Skin?

I can't see what's inside of me. And I'm glad about that! I'm covered with a perfect suit. The real name is skin.

I can never outgrow this suit—it grows with me! Being hot, cold, wet, or dry won't hurt it. It's perfect.

My skin protects me. It keeps germs out. Inside my body, it is very wet. My skin keeps my body from drying out. Sometimes my body gets too warm. Heat escapes through tiny holes called pores. My skin also sweats to cool me off.

What a super covering for my wonderful body!

1. How do you know skin is alive?

_____

2. Tell one way skin protects you.

_____

_____

3. What is another way?

_____

_____

4. What is one way to cool off?

_____

_____

5. Name another way.

_____

_____

TRY THIS: Get a paper towel. Put a blob of paint on it. Press your finger on it. Now press your finger on a piece of paper. This is a fingerprint. Have a friend do the same. See how it is different. No two people have the same!

See How Much I Know!

1. How many muscles do you have? _____

2. What do the cells need besides food? _____

3. What is your cranium? _____

4. What parts take the dirty water out of the blood? _____

5. What muscle churns the food you eat? _____

6. What has millions of air sacs? _____

7. Of what is everything in your body made? _____

8. What takes food and oxygen to your cells? _____

9. What makes everything work? _____

10. What do cells do with food? _____

11. How many bones do you have? _____

12. Of what is your heart made? _____

13. What part of the brain lets you think? _____

14. What keeps your body from drying out? _____

15. What are the two kinds
    of tubes that carry the blood? _____

16. What are the messengers in your body? _____

17. What has four rooms and two pumps? _____

Hm-m-m!

I know!

The Word Box

cortex	lungs	medulla
stomach	nerves	oxygen
burn it	kidneys	blood
cells	over 500	brain
skull	skin	muscles
muscle	hipbone	over 200
arteries	heart	veins

The Mouse in the Jar

Joseph Priestley lit the candle and put the lid on the jar. The candle went out. "Hmm," said Joseph. He put a mouse into the jar. The mouse looked sick . It could not **breathe** right. Hmm, thought Joseph. He opened the jar and let new air in for the mouse.

Joseph Priestley lit the candle and put the jar lid on. The candle went out again. This time he put a mint plant into the jar. He shut the lid tightly. Ten days later he put the mouse into the jar with the mint. The mouse ran around happily. "Aha!" cried Joseph. "The mint plant fixed the air. The mouse can breathe now."

Joseph had discovered something wonderful. He had found out that green plants make **oxygen**. Animals breathe oxygen from the air.

1. The main idea of this story is:

   a. Mice live in jars.
   b. Green plants make oxygen.
   c. Candles burn.

2. Animals get _____ from the air.

   a. water
   b. oxygen
   c. to take air in

3. To breathe means:

   a. to sing a lot
   b. to talk loudly
   c. to take air in

4. When the lid was on the jar, the candle:

   a. burned brightly
   b. stayed the same
   c. went out

5. Planting trees around your house:

   a. helps make fresh air
   b. takes air away
   c. brings mice

Mother Goose

Konrad Lorenz looked at the goose eggs. The goslings were hatching. Lorenz walked away. The newly-hatched goslings followed him. He walked across the grass to the pond. The goslings still followed him. They thought that Konrad Lorenz was their mother.

Konrad Lorenz did some experiments. He found out that goslings will follow anything. Lorenz put a bottle by the next batch of goslings that hatched. He moved the bottle. The goslings went straight to the bottle. They thought it was their mother. Goslings think the first moving thing they see is their mother. Many kinds of birds act this way.

1. The main idea of this story is:

  a. Baby birds find their mothers.
  b. Konrad Lorenz was a goose.
  c. Geese like bottles.

2. A baby goose is a:

  a. gooselet
  b. gosling
  c. duckling

3. Hatching means:

  a. sleeping in an egg
  b. laying eggs
  c. coming out of an egg

4. The goslings followed Konrad because he was:

  a. really their mother
  b. the first moving thing they saw
  c. going swimming

5. The first thing baby birds probably see is:

  a. their mothers
  b. rocks
  c. bottles

FS-32049 Science

Blindfolds on Bats?

Bats come out at night. They fly around in the dark. They hunt for insects to eat. Bats' eyes are very little. Their ears are big.

Donald Griffin learned that bats do not use their eyes to find food. He put blindfolds on bats. He threw insects up into the air. His bats could still catch the insects.

Donald learned that bats squeak as they fly. The "squeak" sound hits the insects. The sound bounces back. The bouncing sound is an echo. The bat has big ears. It hears the echo and finds the insect.

1. The main idea of this story is:

   a. Bats use their eyes to hunt.
   b. Bats use their ears to hunt.
   c. Bats have little ears.

2. Donald Griffin kept bats because:

   a. He wanted to learn about bats.
   b. It was Halloween.
   c. Bats make good pets.

3. An echo is:

   a. a person yelling
   b. a loud noise
   c. a sound that bounces back

4. Donald Griffin found that bats:

   a. do not use their eyes to find food
   b. make no sounds
   c. eat rice

5. A bat could not find food if:

   a. It could make no sound.
   b. It was too dark.
   c. The moon was out.

FS-32049 Science

The Seeing Scientist

A **scientist** must see things. Charles Darwin liked to look at new things. He got a job on a ship. He sailed to new lands on the Beagle.

He walked and he looked. He saw how things were the same. He saw how things were different.

One day he found some strange plants. The leaves crawled. The twigs moved. Charles Darwin wondered, how are these leaves and twigs moving?

Darwin was a scientist. He saw things. He asked questions.

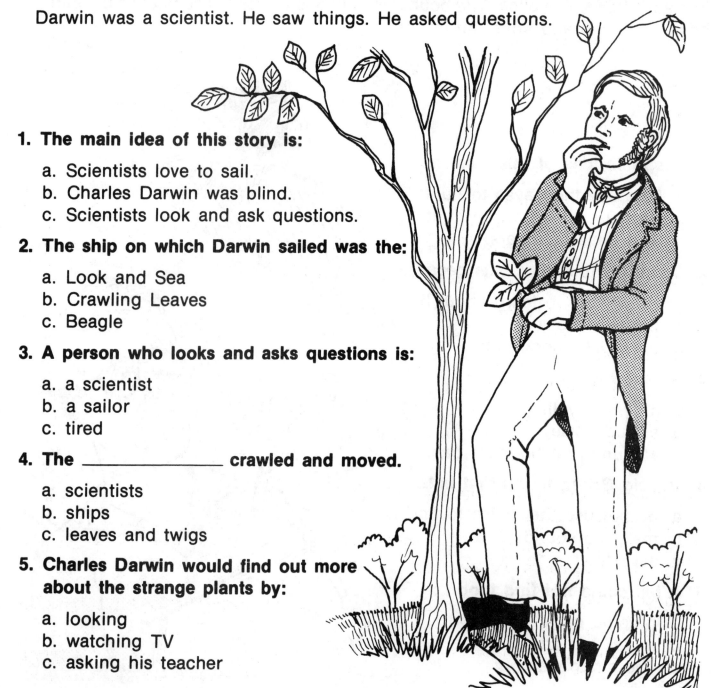

1. The main idea of this story is:

   a. Scientists love to sail.
   b. Charles Darwin was blind.
   c. Scientists look and ask questions.

2. The ship on which Darwin sailed was the:

   a. Look and Sea
   b. Crawling Leaves
   c. Beagle

3. A person who looks and asks questions is:

   a. a scientist
   b. a sailor
   c. tired

4. The _____ crawled and moved.

   a. scientists
   b. ships
   c. leaves and twigs

5. Charles Darwin would find out more about the strange plants by:

   a. looking
   b. watching TV
   c. asking his teacher

FS-32049 Science

What Darwin Found

Charles Darwin had sailed to new lands. On his trips Charles saw new animals. He saw how the animals stayed alive. He found some **insects**. Insects are little animals with six legs. They were hiding. The insects were the same color as leaves. The insects were the same shape as leaves. Some were the same shape as twigs.

Darwin wondered why these insects looked like plants.

A bird hopped by. It was looking for food to feed its babies. Darwin watched. The bird flew away to look somewhere else. Now Darwin knew the answer to his question.

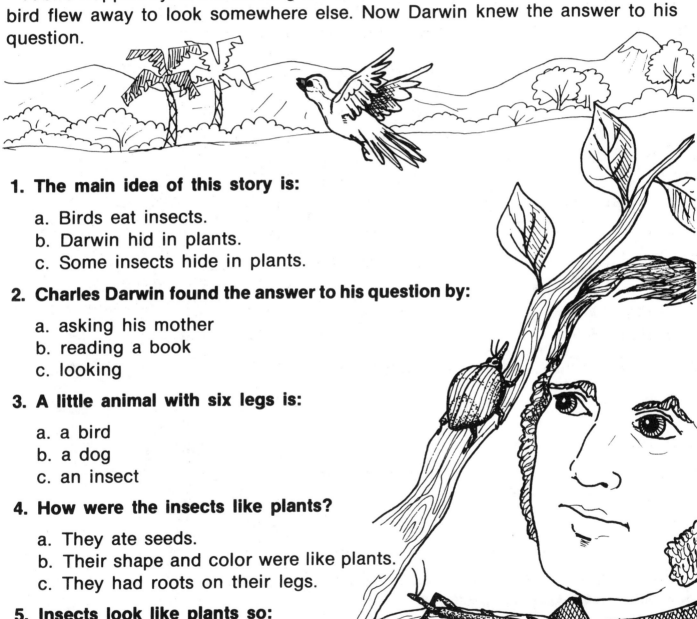

1. The main idea of this story is:

   a. Birds eat insects.
   b. Darwin hid in plants.
   c. Some insects hide in plants.

2. Charles Darwin found the answer to his question by:

   a. asking his mother
   b. reading a book
   c. looking

3. A little animal with six legs is:

   a. a bird
   b. a dog
   c. an insect

4. How were the insects like plants?

   a. They ate seeds.
   b. Their shape and color were like plants.
   c. They had roots on their legs.

5. Insects look like plants so:

   a. Birds cannot eat them.
   b. Birds can find them.
   c. They can find food.

   FS-32049 Science

Energy from the Sun

The sun is up. The day is warm and light. The sun goes down. The night is cool and dark. Heat and light are kinds of energy. Heat and light come from the sun. Green plant leaves catch the **energy** from the sun.

Make two paper leaves. Make them about as big as your hand. Color the leaves dark, dark green with a crayon. Put one out in the bright sunlight. Put the other one in the shade. After about one hour, touch the leaves. The one in the shade is cool. Feel the heat energy from the one in the sun. The paper leaf has the energy from the sun in it.

1. The main idea of this story is:

    a. Heat and light energy come from the sun.
    b. Plants need light to grow.
    c. It gets warm when the sun goes down.

2. The sun has:

    a. two leaves
    b. two colors
    c. two kinds of energy

3. Touch means:

    a. feel
    b. see
    c. taste

4. The leaf in the shade is:

    a. hot
    b. cool
    c. brown

5. Plants need sunlight because:

    a. They need energy to grow.
    b. It is dark at night.
    c. The roots grow down.

FS-32049 Science

Green Plants and Oxygen

Monday morning Mr. Lombird said, "Open your books to page 23. It says, 'Joseph Priestley found that green plants make oxygen.' You will have a test on this on Thursday."

Hubley looked at the **aquarium** on the window sill. The sun was shining through it. Hubley saw little bubbles coming from the plants. He got an idea. Hubley dropped a little jar into the aquarium. Next, he turned the jar filled with water upside down over a plant. He put some rocks around the jar to hold it above the plant. The little bubbles from the plant went up into the jar. He went back to his desk to read page 23.

Three days later Hubley looked at the jar. A lot of the water was gone. A big bubble of oxygen was in the upside down jar. It was the day of the test. Hubley looked at question number one. It said, "Tell how to get oxygen from a green plant." Hubley smiled.

1. The main idea of this story is:

a. taking a test
b. getting oxygen from a plant
c. reading books

2. The big bubble coming from the plant was:

a. oxygen
b. water
c. hot air

3. A tank filled with water to keep fish is:

a. a bathtub
b. a bubble bath
c. an aquarium

4. It took _____ days to get the bubble of oxygen.

a. 2
b. 3
c. 4

5. The plants got the energy they need to make oxygen from the:

a. sun
b. teacher
c. water

FS-32049 Science

The Better to Hear You With

Animals with big ears can hear well. You can pretend that your ears are bigger than they are. Cup your hand behind your ear like this:

Get a long ruler and a watch that ticks.
Don't let the ruler touch your ear.
Put the ruler next to your ear.
Move the watch away until you cannot hear it tick.
Mark the place on the ruler with a piece of tape.
Now try it without your hand behind your ear.
Mark this distance on the ruler, too.

You will find that you can hear the watch farther away when you hold up your hand. Your hand makes your ear seem bigger. You can hear better.

1. **The main idea of this story is:**
   a. Animals see better at night.
   b. You can hear better at night.
   c. Big ears help you to hear better.

2. **You can hear better with your:**
   a. finger in your ear
   b. hand behind your ear
   c. hand over your eyes

3. **When you find the distance, you find:**
   a. how big
   b. how far
   c. hand over your eyes

4. **Find out how far away the watch is with a**
   a. gas meter
   b. meteor
   c. long ruler

5. **A rabbit can hear _____ a person can.**
   a. better than
   b. the same as
   c. not as well as

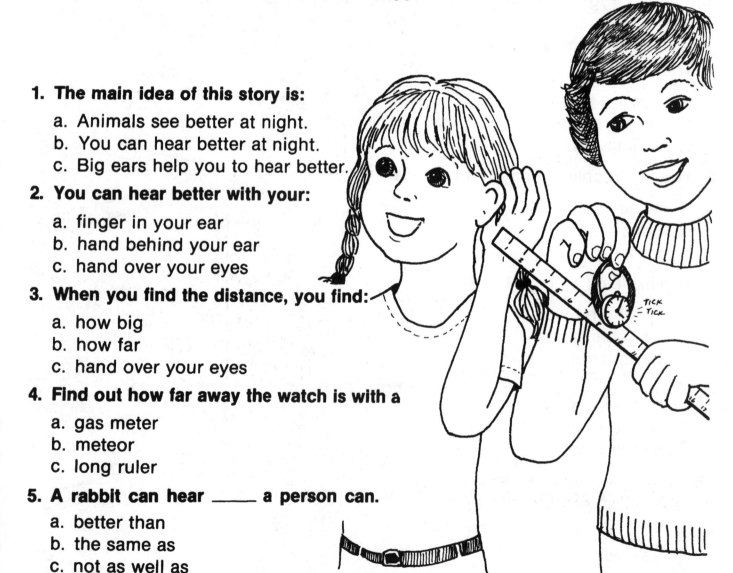

102

FS-32049 Science

The Cat's In the Cupboard

Cats hunt at night. They have eyes that can see in the dark. Look into the cat's eyes. The black part in the middle is the **pupil**. Put the cat in the sunlight. His pupils will get very small. Bring him back into the room. His pupils will get larger. The pupil is a hole. It lets light into the eye. Eyes need light to see. At night there is not much light. For one minute, put the cat into a closet. Take him out and look into his eyes. Now his pupils are very big. They let in all of the light they can. The cat can see in the dark.

1. **The main idea of this story is:**

   a. Cats' eyes change.
   b. Cats live in closets.
   c. Cats sleep at night.

2. **At night a cat's pupil:**

   a. is little
   b. turns blue
   c. is big

3. **The hole that lets light in is:**

   a. blue or yellow
   b. always big
   c. the pupil

4. **The cat's pupils will get small:**

   a. in the sunlight
   b. in the room
   c. in the closet

5. **Cats hunt mice, so you can tell that mice come out:**

   a. for recess
   b. at night
   c. in the daytime

FS-32049 Science

Review

1. Heat and light energy come from:

a. the air b. food c. the sun

2. What is a bouncing sound called?

a. a rainbow b. a squeak c. an echo

3. The pupil of the eye lets in _____.

a. music b. light c. sounds

4. Some insects hide themselves by looking like:

a. birds and frogs
b. leaves and twigs
c. snow and rain

5. Scientists:

a. live on boats
b. know everything
c. look and ask questions

6. Green plants make:

a. oxygen b. smog   c. sunlight

7. An _____ is a little animal with six legs.

a. elephant   b. insect   c. orange

8. Distance tells you:

a. how many b. how far c. how old

9. An aquarium is filled with:

a. water b. dirt c. air

10. _____ breathe oxygen from the air.

a. plants b. animals c. stars

11. Some insects hide. They look like:

a. parts of plants b. mice c. Charles Darwin

12. At night a cat's pupils get:

a. big b. little c. blue

FS-32049 Science

Answer Key

Mammals

If you have ever seen a dog, cat, mouse, or cow, or looked at yourself in a mirror, you have seen a mammal. Mammals come in many shapes and sizes. All mammals, however, share special traits.

Mammals are the only animals that nurse their young. This means that the babies are fed with the mother's milk.

Mammals are often very caring parents. They protect and train their young. One or both parents care for the babies. The young learn mostly by imitating, or copying, their parents.

Mammals are warm-blooded. Their body temperature stays about the same even though the air temperature around them changes.

All mammals have hair at some time in their lives. In some whales, though, hair is present only before birth.

Finally, mammals have larger, more complex brains than other animals. They are thought to be the most intelligent of all animals.

Write the answer to each question.

1. What do mammals feed their newborn babies?
   The babies are fed with the mother's milk.

2. Who cares for the baby mammals?
   One or both parents care for the babies.

3. Young mammals imitate their parents. What does *imitate* mean?
   Imitate means to copy.

4. Mammals are warm-blooded. What does this mean? **Their body temperature stays about the same even though the air temperature around them changes.**

5. Name two mammals. **Answers vary.**

Try This! On the back of this paper, list five ways mammals differ from other creatures.

Page 1

Natural Habitats of Mammals

Animals live in many kinds of surroundings. The place where an animal lives in nature is called its natural habitat. There are many kinds of natural habitats. Each animal is best suited to the habitat in which it lives.

The **ocean** is the watery home of whales, dolphins, porpoises, and seals. Elephants, lions, giraffes, and zebras live in grassy plains called **grasslands**. Mammals that live in the **forest** include wolves, bears, deer, and raccoons. Polar bears, arctic hares, caribou, and musk oxen live in the cold climate of the **polar regions**.

1. List each mammal under its natural habitat.

bear	zebra	caribou	lion
musk ox	dolphin	raccoon	wolf
porpoise	whale	polar bear	seal
elephant	arctic hare	giraffe	deer

Ocean	Grasslands	Forest	Polar Regions
whale	elephant	bear	musk ox
dolphin	zebra	raccoon	arctic hare
porpoise	giraffe	wolf	caribou
seal	lion	deer	polar bear

2. Draw a picture showing one of the above animals in its natural habitat.

Pictures will vary.

Try This! The desert is another habitat. List four animals that live there.

Page 2

The Blue Whale

The blue whale is the largest animal in the world. It is a sea mammal. It can grow up to 100 feet long and weigh as much as 100 tons.

Unlike most mammals which have four legs, the blue whale does not have any legs. Instead, it has two front flippers. It uses its flippers for steering and balancing while swimming.

The blue whale has no teeth. Instead, it has thin plates, called baleen, that hang from the roof of its mouth. The baleen looks like the teeth of a comb and acts as a strainer. When the blue whale eats, it opens its huge mouth and takes in large amounts of water and krill, a tiny shrimplike animal. The water is then forced out through the baleen and the krill is left behind to be swallowed.

Write the answer to each question.

1. What is the length and weight of a blue whale?
   A blue whale can be 100 feet long and can weigh as much as 100 tons.

2. What does the blue whale use its flippers for while it is swimming?
   It uses its flippers for steering and balancing.

3. What hangs from the roof of the blue whale's mouth?
   Thin plates, called baleen, hang from the roof of its mouth.

4. What does the blue whale eat? **The blue whale eats krill.**

5. Can blue whales chew food? **No, blue whales cannot chew food.**

Try This! Write five more facts about the blue whale. A library book or encyclopedia will help you.

Page 3

Mammal Hunt

Use the pictures to help you write the answers to the riddles.

1. I have a hump on my back that I use for storing fat.
   camel

2. I live in the ocean. I am the largest of all mammals.
   blue whale

3. I am the only flying mammal. **bat**

4. I have a long snout and sticky tongue. I mainly eat ants.
   anteater

5. I use my sharp front teeth to cut down trees. My broad, flat tail looks like a paddle. **beaver**

6. I am the largest land mammal. I have a trunk and tusks.
   elephant

7. My fingers help me hold things. I like to swing from tree branches.
   monkey

8. I sometimes wear "shoes." I provide transportation and pleasure for many people. **horse**

Try This! Write a riddle about another mammal. Trade with a friend.

Page 4

Animal Behavior

The behavior of an animal is the way in which the animal acts. There are two types of animal behavior.

Instinct is behavior that the animal knows from birth. It is behavior that the animal does automatically without thinking about it. A bird building a nest, for example, acts from instinct. No one had to teach the bird what to do.

Learned behavior is something that an animal learns to do. It is behavior that an animal would not do naturally. For example, a circus seal that balances a ball on its nose does so because someone taught it to do the trick. Balancing a ball is not part of the seal's natural behavior.

Write each phrase under the correct heading.
- a bird feeding her young
- a bear hibernating in winter
- a horse performing in a horse show
- a skunk spraying in danger
- a dog catching a stick
- a porpoise jumping through a hoop

Instinct
1. a bird feeding her young
2. a bear hibernating in winter
3. a skunk spraying in danger

Learned Behavior
1. a horse performing in a horse show
2. a dog catching a stick
3. a porpoise jumping through a hoop

Try This! If you could teach an animal to do a trick, which animal would you choose and what would the trick be? Write your answer.

Page 5

Mammal Communication

Mammals can communicate. Although they do not talk as people do, they share information. Mammals are born knowing how to communicate with mammals of their own kind.

Some mammals use sound signals to communicate. Dogs and wolves bark. Lions use low coughs. Chimpanzees make sounds that have specific meanings. Prairie dogs whistle to warn one another of danger.

Scent is another way mammals communicate. A bear, for example, leaves its scent around its territory by plastering mud on trees and rubbing its back against the mud. Its hairs rub off and leave a scent indicating the bear's presence.

Some mammals communicate with their face and body. Wolves draw back their upper lip and show their fangs when in danger. Gorillas beat their chest with their fists when they are angry.

Touch is another form of animal communication. Horses, deer, and cattle show affection by nuzzling, licking, and neck rubbing. Chimpanzees sometimes hug to show affection.

Circle **True** or **False** for each statement below.

1. Some mammals use sound signals to communicate. **(True)** False
2. Mammals must be taught how to communicate. True **(False)**
3. Bears communicate using scent messages. **(True)** False
4. A wolf's face changes when it senses danger. **(True)** False
5. No mammal communicates by touching. True **(False)**
6. Gorillas sometimes show they are angry. **(True)** False
7. Horses never show affection. True **(False)**
8. Prairie dogs whistle when there is danger. **(True)** False

Try This! Write three ways that a dog or cat can communicate with its owner.

Page 6

Mammal Report

Choose a mammal for your report. Complete the sentences.

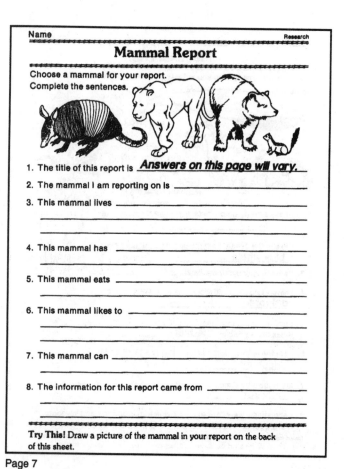

1. The title of this report is *Answers on this page will vary.*
2. The mammal I am reporting on is _____
3. This mammal lives _____
4. This mammal has _____
5. This mammal eats _____
6. This mammal likes to _____
7. This mammal can _____
8. The information for this report came from _____

Try This! Draw a picture of the mammal in your report on the back of this sheet.

Page 7

Mammal Observation Sheet

Observe means to watch or study. Select a mammal to observe. Observe your mammal at different times of the day. Try to find out how it eats and sleeps. Write your observations on the lines below.

Answers on this page will vary.

1. The animal I observed was a _____
2. The place where I observed the animal was _____
3. The animal I observed did the following:
   In the morning _____
   Around noontime _____
   In the afternoon _____
4. This is how the animal moved: _____
5. This animal ate _____
6. The noises that this animal made were _____
7. The animal slept _____

Try This! Write a paragraph describing the animal you observed.

Page 8

Answer Key

What Is a Bird?

A bird is an animal with feathers. Feathers protect a bird's skin and help it keep warm. Feathers also help to waterproof a bird's body.

A bird has two legs and a hard beak. It also has many bones that are hollow like a straw. These bones make the bird lighter and better able to fly. Some birds such as the penguin, though, cannot fly.

Every bird hatches from an egg. The egg is kept warm by the father or mother bird. When the young bird hatches, it is usually fed by its parents.

Write the answers.

1. List three ways feathers help a bird.
   Feathers protect a bird's skin, help it keep warm, and waterproof its body.

2. How do hollow bones help birds?
   Hollow bones make the bird lighter and better able to fly.

3. Name one bird that cannot fly. **A penguin cannot fly.**

4. Who usually cares for a bird when it hatches?
   When a bird hatches, it is usually cared for by its parents.

5. What is your favorite bird? Why is it your favorite?
   Answers vary.

Try This! List as many birds as you can. Try to name at least ten.

Page 9

Birds and Their Nests

Use words from the Word Box to fill in the blanks.

Word Box			
beaks	buildings	holes	lined
build	hatched	nests	sticks

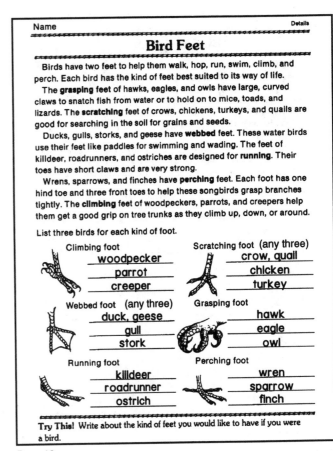

eagle

Most birds build nests to hold their eggs and protect their young. Baby birds are hatched and fed in the nest.

Robins, goldfinches, and sparrows make bowl-shaped nests called open nests. The nests are made of grass, twigs, and leaves, and 1. **lined** with mud.

robin

Pigeons, eagles, and ospreys build stick nests. They build a platform of 2. **sticks** and twigs high up in a tree or on a cliff.

Many birds use mud to make nests. Flamingos use their 3. **beaks** to scrape mud into a mound. Swallows 4. **build** nests of mud mixed with straw and grass, and lined with feathers. You can find swallow nests on cliffs or attached to 5. **buildings** .

flamingo

Woodpeckers find old trees and use their beaks to make 6. **holes** for their nests. Chickadees, wrens, and owls use old woodpecker holes for their 7. **nests** .

woodpecker

The cowbird does not build a nest at all. Instead it lays its eggs in the nest of a smaller bird. The egg is 8. **hatched** and raised by its "foster parents."

Try This! Birds know how to build nests by instinct. Name two things you can do that you did not have to learn.

Page 10

Bird Beaks

Birds use their beaks to eat, take care of their babies, build nests, and protect themselves.

1. A **grosbeak** has a very strong, cone-shaped beak which it uses for cracking seeds.

2. The **spoonbill** uses its spoon-shaped bill to sweep back and forth in water to find food.

3. A **woodpecker** hunts insects by drilling into trees with its thin, pointed beak.

4. The **golden eagle** has a hooked beak that it uses for tearing its prey.

5. The **brown creeper** uses its small, slender beak to search under bark for insects.

6. The beak of the **nighthawk** opens wide and traps insects in midair.

Using the clues from above, write the name of each bird under its picture.

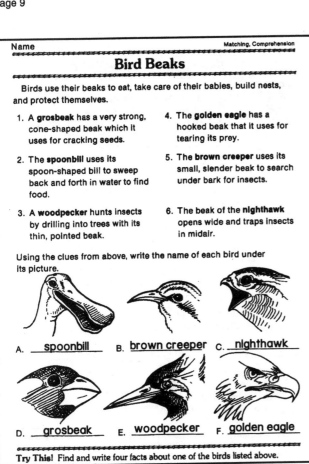

A. **spoonbill**   B. **brown creeper**   C. **nighthawk**

D. **grosbeak**   E. **woodpecker**   F. **golden eagle**

Try This! Find and write four facts about one of the birds listed above.

Page 11

Bird Feet

Birds have two feet to help them walk, hop, run, swim, climb, and perch. Each bird has the kind of feet best suited to its way of life.

The **grasping** feet of hawks, eagles, and owls have large, curved claws to snatch fish from water or to hold on to mice, toads, and lizards. The **scratching** feet of crows, chickens, turkeys, and quails are good for searching in the soil for grains and seeds.

Ducks, gulls, storks, and geese have **webbed** feet. These water birds use their feet like paddles for swimming and wading. The feet of killdeer, roadrunners, and ostriches are designed for **running**. Their toes have short claws and are very strong.

Wrens, sparrows, and finches have **perching** feet. Each foot has one hind toe and three front toes to help these songbirds grasp branches tightly. The **climbing** feet of woodpeckers, parrots, and creepers help them get a good grip on tree trunks as they climb up, down, or around.

List three birds for each kind of foot.

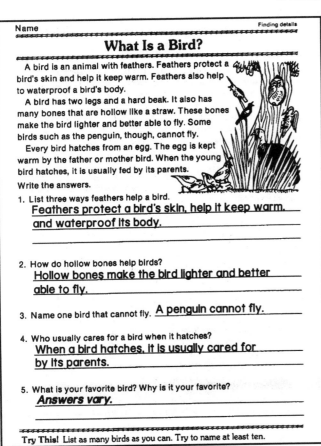

Climbing foot
woodpecker
parrot
creeper

Scratching foot (any three)
crow, quail
chicken
turkey

Webbed foot (any three)
duck, geese
gull
stork

Grasping foot
hawk
eagle
owl

Running foot
killdeer
roadrunner
ostrich

Perching foot
wren
sparrow
finch

Try This! Write about the kind of feet you would like to have if you were a bird.

Page 12

FS-32049 Science

Answer Key

Name   Compare and contrast

Comparing Birds

The roadrunner lives in the deserts of western North America. The adult bird is twenty-three inches long and has brown and tan feathers. Its powerful beak can kill snakes and scorpions, but lizards are its main food. A road-runner builds its nest in a cactus or bush. The female lays two to nine eggs at a time.

The ruby-throated hummingbird lives in eastern North America. It grows to be only three and one-half inches long. It uses its long, pointed beak to sip flower nectar, and catch insects and spiders. The mother hummingbird usually lays two, pea-sized, white eggs in a nest about the size of a quarter.

Write the phrases below under the correct heading.

- desert bird
- very small bird
- long, pointed beak
- powerful beak
- sips nectar
- eats lizards
- eastern North America
- western North America

Roadrunner	Ruby-throated Hummingbird
desert bird	very small bird
powerful beak	long, pointed beak
eats lizards	sips nectar
western North America	eastern North America

Try This! Compare two other North American birds. Write four phrases to describe each.

Page 13

Name   Reading a chart

State Birds

Phil was working on a report about state birds. In an almanac, he was surprised to find that many states had the same state bird. Here is a chart of some of the state birds that Phil learned about.

Bluebird - Idaho, New York, Nevada, Missouri	**Robin** - Michigan, Connecticut, Wisconsin
Goldfinch - New Jersey, Washington, Iowa	**Cardinal** - Illinois, Ohio, Kentucky, Indiana, North Carolina, Virginia, West Virginia
Chickadee - Maine, Massachusetts	

On the line beside each bird, write the number of states that have that bird as their state bird.

Goldfinch __3__   Robin __3__

Cardinal __7__   Chickadee __2__   Bluebird __4__

Write the answers to the following questions.
1. What is the state bird of Maine? __chickadee__
2. How many states have the goldfinch as their state bird? __3__
3. Which states have the bluebird as their state bird? __Idaho, New York, Nevada, Missouri__
4. How many states have the cardinal as their state bird? __7__
5. What is the state bird of Wisconsin? __Robin__

Try This! Paint a picture of your state bird.

Page 14

Name   Context clues

Bird Migration

Some birds like the blue jay, quail, and cardinal stay in one area all year long. But many birds migrate, or move from one place to another, when the seasons change. When the weather turns cold and food is hard to find, these birds fly south to warmer areas. When spring comes, they fly north again to build their nests.

Some birds migrate during the day, but many travel in the darkness of night for protection. Ducks, geese, hawks, and swallows migrate during the day, while timid songbirds such as warblers and thrushes travel at night.

Migration is full of dangers for the winged travelers. Often birds crash into high objects such as tall buildings or power lines. Sometimes birds fly into storms or strong winds and do not survive.

How do migrating birds find their way? Birds have an excellent sense of direction. Scientists think that birds may use the sun, stars, winds, or the shape of the land below to guide them.

Complete the sentences by filling in the missing letters.

1. When birds travel due to seasonal changes, it is called **m i g r a t i o n**.
2. Many birds fly south when the **w e a t h e r** becomes cold.
3. Some birds use the darkness of night for **p r o t e c t i o n**.
4. Most songbirds travel at **n i g h t**.
5. Birds have a good sense of **d i r e c t i o n**.
6. Migration is full of **d a n g e r s** for birds.
7. Sometimes birds crash into tall **b u i l d i n g s**.

Try This! If you were a migrating bird, would you travel at night or during the day? Explain why.

Page 15

Name   Sentence completion

John James Audubon

John James Audubon was born on April 26, 1785. He was one of the first people to study and paint the birds of North America.

As a boy living in France he learned to hunt and to play the violin, but he preferred to go on hikes and collect birds' nests and eggs. Before he was 18, he had made about 200 drawings of birds.

In 1803 Audubon came to America. Later he married Lucy Bakewell. She believed that John was a great artist. She worked as a teacher to support the family. John traveled through the American countryside, watching, collecting, and painting birds.

Audubon's paintings were published in a book. They showed life-sized birds nesting, feeding, fighting, and flying. He mixed pencil, watercolor, crayon, chalk, and ink to make his birds look real.

Accept any reasonable answers:
Use the facts above to finish each sentence.
1. John Audubon __was born on April 26, 1785.__
2. When John was young __he liked to hike and collect birds' nests and eggs.__
3. In 1803 __Audubon came to America.__
4. Lucy believed __that John was a great artist.__
5. To make his paintings look real, John __mixed pencil, watercolor, crayon, chalk and ink.__
6. Audubon's paintings __were published in a book.__

Try This! Write three questions you wish you could ask John James Audubon about his life.

Page 16

FS-32049 Science

Answer Key

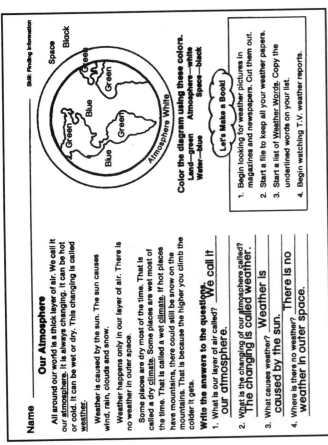

Name _____

Skill: Finding Information

Our Atmosphere

All around our world is a thick layer of air. We call it our atmosphere. It is always changing. It can be hot or cold. It can be wet or dry. This changing is called weather.

Weather is caused by the sun. The sun causes wind, rain, clouds and snow.

Weather happens only in our layer of air. There is no weather in outer space.

Some places are dry most of the time. That is called a dry climate. Some places are wet most of the time. That is called a wet climate. If hot places have mountains, there could still be snow on the mountains. That is because the higher you climb the colder it gets.

Write the answers to the questions.
1. What is our layer of air called? We call it our atmosphere.
2. What is the changing of our atmosphere called? The changing is called weather.
3. What causes weather? Weather is caused by the sun.
4. Where is there no weather? There is no weather in outer space.

Color the diagram using these colors.
Land—green   Atmosphere—white
Water—blue   Space—black

Space — Black
Green
Blue
Green
Green
Blue
Green
Atmosphere White

Let's Make a Book!
1. Begin looking for weather pictures in magazines and newspapers. Cut them out.
2. Start a file to keep all your weather papers.
3. Start a list of Weather Words. Copy the underlined words on your list.
4. Begin watching T.V. weather reports.

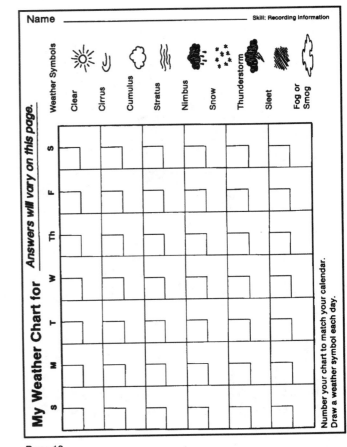

Name _____

Skill: Recording Information

My Weather Chart for _____ *Answers will vary on this page.*

Weather Symbols

Clear
Cirrus
Cumulus
Stratus
Nimbus
Snow
Thunderstorm
Sleet
Fog or Smog

S	M	T	W	Th	F	S

Number your chart to match your calendar.
Draw a weather symbol each day.

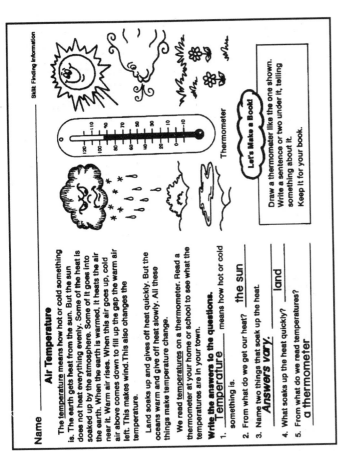

Name _____

Skill: Finding Information

Air Temperature

The temperature means how hot or cold something is. The earth gets heat from the sun. But the sun does not heat everything evenly. Some of the heat is soaked up by the atmosphere. Some of it goes into the earth. When the earth is warmed, it heats the air near it. Warm air rises. When this air goes up, cold air above comes down to fill up the gap the warm air left. This makes wind. This also changes the temperature.

Land soaks up and gives off heat quickly. But the oceans warm and give off heat slowly. All these things make temperature change.

We read temperatures on a thermometer. Read a thermometer at your home or school to see what the temperatures are in your town.

Thermometer

Write the answers to the questions.
1. Temperature means how hot or cold something is.
2. From what do we get our heat? the sun
3. Name two things that soak up the heat. Answers vary.
4. What soaks up heat quickly? land
5. From what do we read temperatures? a thermometer

Let's Make a Book!
Draw a thermometer like the one shown. Write a sentence or two under it, telling something about it.
Keep it for your book.

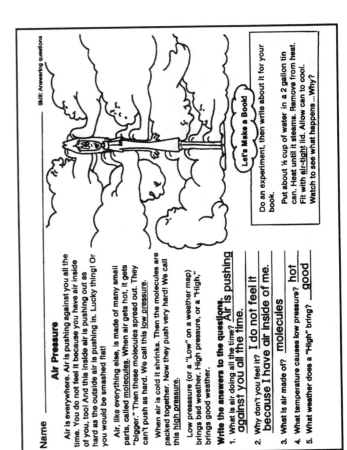

Name _____

Skill: Answering questions

Air Pressure

Air is everywhere. Air is pushing against you all the time. You do not feel it because you have air inside of you, too! And this inside air is pushing out as hard as the outside air is pushing in. Lucky thing! Or you would be smashed flat!

Air, like everything else, is made of many small parts, called molecules. When air gets hot, it gets "bigger." Then these molecules spread out. They can't push as hard. We call this low pressure.

When air is cold it shrinks. Then the molecules are packed together. Now they push very hard! We call this high pressure.

Low pressure (or a "Low" on a weather map) brings bad weather. High pressure, or a "High," brings good weather.

Write the answers to the questions.
1. What is air doing all the time? Air is pushing against you all the time.
2. Why don't you feel it? I do not feel it because I have air inside of me.
3. What is air made of? molecules
4. What temperature causes low pressure? hot
5. What weather does a "High" bring? good

Let's Make a Book!
Do an experiment, then write about it for your book.

Put about ¼ cup of water in a 2 gallon tin can. Heat until it steams. Remove from heat. Fit with air-tight lid. Allow can to cool. Watch to see what happens...Why?

FS-32049 Science

Answer Key

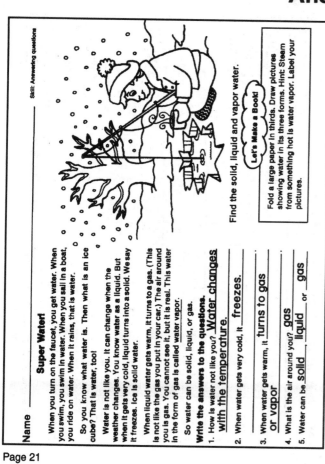

Skill: Answering questions

Name _____

Super Water!

When you turn on the faucet, you get water. When you swim, you swim in water. When you sail in a boat, you ride on water. When it rains, that is water.

So you know what water is. Then what is an ice cube? That is water, too!

Water is not like you. It can change when the weather changes. You know water as a liquid. But when it gets very cold, liquid turns into a solid. We say it freezes. Ice is solid water.

When liquid water gets warm, it turns to a gas. (This is not like the gas you put in your car.) The air around you is gas. You cannot see it, but it is real. This water in the form of gas is called water vapor.

So water can be solid, liquid, or gas.

Write the answers to the questions.

1. How is water not like you? __Water changes with the temperature.__

2. When water gets very cold, it __freezes.__

3. When water gets warm, it __turns to gas or vapor__

4. What is the air around you? __gas__

5. Water can be __solid__ __liquid__ or __gas__

Let's Make a Book!

Find the solid, liquid and vapor water.

Fold a large paper in thirds. Draw pictures showing water in its three forms. Hint: Steam from something hot is water vapor. Label your pictures.

Skill: Finding facts

Name _____

How Clouds Form

Clouds are made of tiny drops of water and specks of dust. Some clouds are made of tiny bits of ice. These drops or bits are very tiny! More than 100 million could fit in a teaspoon!

The sun shines on the oceans, rivers and lakes. When the water is warmed, it is changed to a gas called water vapor. We say, "It evaporated."

Warm air always rises, so this vapor goes up. The upper air is cooler. Now the water vapor bumps into specks of dust that are cold.

It becomes liquid again. We say, "It condenses." Billions of these drops come together to form a cloud.

Write the answers to the questions.

1. What are clouds made of? __Clouds are made of tiny drops of water and specks of dust.__

2. What sentence shows you how tiny they are? __More than 100 million could fit in a teaspoon__

3. When liquid water became vapor, it __evaporated.__

4. Where does warm air always go? __up__

5. When vapor becomes liquid, it __condenses__

Let's Make a Book!

Do some Tear-Paste Art:

Needed: 12" x 18" blue paper
Scraps—all colors
Paste
No scissors!

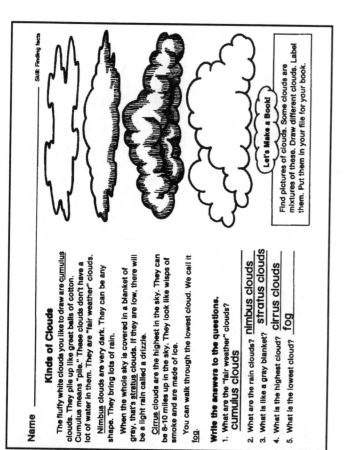

Skill: Finding facts

Name _____

Kinds of Clouds

The fluffy white clouds you like to draw are cumulus clouds. They pile up like great balls of cotton. Cumulus means "pile." These clouds don't have a lot of water in them. They are "fair weather" clouds.

Nimbus clouds are very dark. They can be any shape. They bring lots of rain.

When the whole sky is covered in a blanket of gray, that's stratus clouds. If they are low, there will be a light rain called a drizzle.

Cirrus clouds are the highest in the sky. They can be 8–10 miles up in the sky. They look like wisps of smoke and are made of ice.

You can walk through the lowest cloud. We call it fog.

Write the answers to the questions.

1. What are the "fair weather" clouds? __cumulus clouds__

2. What are the rain clouds? __nimbus clouds__

3. What is like a gray blanket? __stratus clouds__

4. What is the highest cloud? __cirrus clouds__

5. What is the lowest cloud? __fog__

Let's Make a Book!

Find pictures of clouds. Some clouds are mixtures of these. Draw different clouds. Label them. Put them in your file for your book.

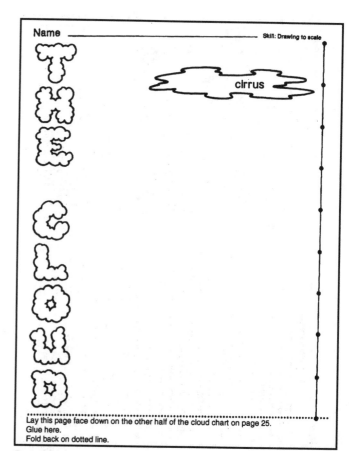

Name _____

Skill: Drawing to scale

THE CLOUDS

cirrus

Lay this page face down on the other half of the cloud chart on page 25.
Glue here.
Fold back on dotted line.

Answer Key

Page 25

Name _____ Skill: Drawing to scale

Name _____ Skill: Drawing to scale

Glue other half of cloud chart here.

Fold it back.

Your chart will be 17 inches high.

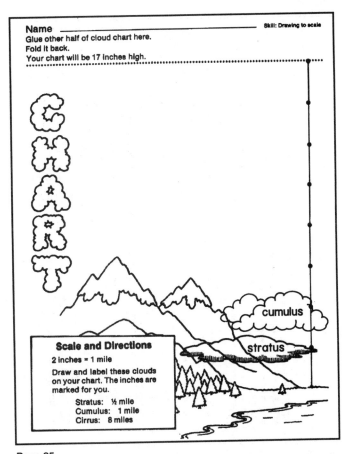

CHART

cumulus

stratus

Scale and Directions

2 inches = 1 mile

Draw and label these clouds on your chart. The inches are marked for you.

Stratus: ½ mile
Cumulus: 1 mile
Cirrus: 8 miles

Page 26

Name _____ Skill: Answering questions

Smog

Smog is a man-made kind of weather. Years ago it was unknown.

Smog is found hanging over many large cities of the world. The word "smog" is made of two words: smoke and fog.

Large cities have many industries. Industries give off smoke. Cities have many cars and buses. They give off exhaust.

When water evaporates, it collects and condenses on bits of dirt in the air. In large cities where the air is dirty, this makes smog.

Smog is a problem. It is bad for our eyes and lungs. We are always looking for ways to rid ourselves of smog.

Write answers to the questions.

1. Where is smog found? <u>Smog is found hanging over many large cities of the world.</u>

2. What two words make the word "smog"? <u>smoke and fog</u>

3. What makes the smoke? <u>Industries, exhaust from cars and buses make smoke.</u>

4. What does water vapor need to condense? <u>It condenses on bits of dirt in the air.</u>

Let's Make a Book!

You are the mayor of a large, smoggy city. You must get rid of this problem. What is your plan? Write it down for your book.

Page 27

Name _____ Skill: Finding facts

The Water Cycle

The dark clouds begin to rain. The rain falls on the grass and the streets, making puddles. It falls on the hills, running down in little streams. They flow into lakes and on to the ocean.

The rain is over. Out peeks the sun. The water in the puddles, streams, lakes, and ocean gets warm. It changes to vapor, like steam rising out of a boiling teakettle. It disappears into the air.

Warm air rises, so up it goes. The air is cooler here. There are specks of dust. When the vapor hits a cool speck, it sticks to it and condenses. These bits of dust and water drops come together to make clouds. When they are heavy with water, down comes the rain again.

Do you see why it is called a cycle?

Write the answers to the questions.

1. What falls from the dark clouds? <u>rain</u>

2. What warms the water? <u>sun</u>

3. When water is warmed, what happens? <u>It changes to vapor.</u>

4. When vapor hits a cool speck, what does it do? <u>It condenses.</u>

Let's Make a Book!

Do an experiment. Then write about it for your book:

Put a cup of water in a flat pan. Heat to boiling. Put ice cubes in a small pan. Hold it over the steam. Watch the water cycle!

Page 28

Name _____ Skill: Conceptualizing water cycle

Water Cycle Wheel is completed as directed.

The Water Cycle Wheel

cut out

cut out

cut out

Color.   Cut out the parts marked.   Use with page 29.

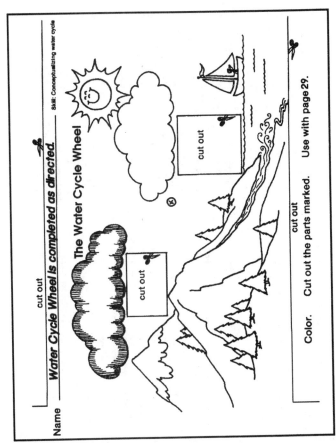

FS-32049 Science

Answer Key

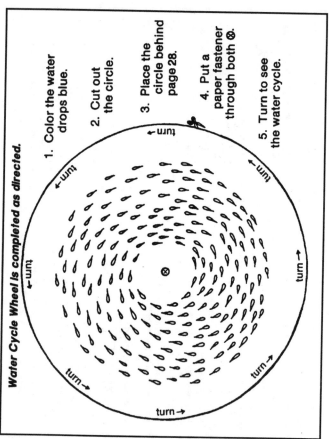

Water Cycle Wheel is completed as directed.

1. Color the water drops blue.
2. Cut out the circle.
3. Place the circle behind page 28.
4. Put a paper fastener through both ⊗.
5. Turn to see the water cycle.

Page 29

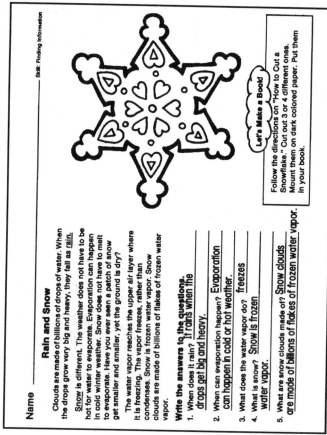

Name _____

Rain and Snow

Clouds are made of billions of drops of water. When the drops grow very big and heavy, they fall as <u>rain</u>.

Snow is different. The weather does not have to be hot for water to evaporate. Evaporation can happen in cold winter weather. Snow does not have to melt to evaporate. Have you ever seen a patch of snow get smaller and smaller, yet the ground is dry?

The water vapor reaches the upper air layer where it is freezing. The vapor freezes, rather than condenses. Snow is frozen water vapor. Snow clouds are made of billions of flakes of frozen water vapor.

Write the answers to the questions.

1. When does it rain? <u>It rains when the drops get big and heavy.</u>

2. When can evaporation happen? <u>Evaporation can happen in cold or hot weather.</u>

3. What does the water vapor do? <u>freezes</u>

4. What is snow? <u>Snow is frozen water vapor.</u>

5. What are snow clouds made of? <u>Snow clouds are made of billions of flakes of frozen water vapor.</u>

Let's Make a Book!

Follow the directions on "How to Cut a Snowflake." Cut out 3 or 4 different ones. Mount them on dark colored paper. Put them in your book.

Page 30

Name _____

A snowflake is completed as directed

How to Cut a Snowflake

All snowflakes have 6 sides. No two are alike!

1. Start with a square. (Rectangle works, too)
2. Fold in half.
3. Fold in half again. Open back to step 2.
4. Fold side to center fold line. Open back to step 2.
5. Press finger at A. Hold in place. throw away / keep / Cut
6. Fold corner B to touch line C.
7. Fold up side D to line up evenly with side E.
8.
9. Turn to put point F at top. Cut a "door" in the "tepee."
10. Cut out pieces along all four sides.
11. Unfold.

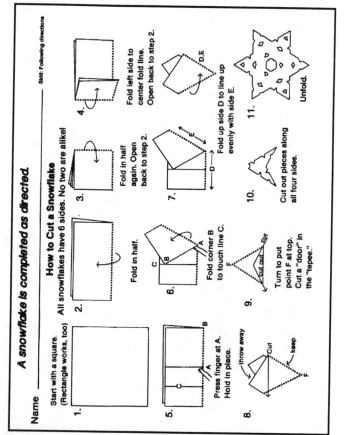

Page 31

Name _____

Hail, Sleet and Glaze

<u>Hail</u> looks like marbles made of ice. They can be bigger than baseballs! A hailstone starts as a raindrop in a thundercloud. It freezes and falls within the big cloud. Then it is lifted by wind to freeze and fall again. Each time it grows bigger. When it is too heavy to be lifted again, it falls to the ground. Hailstorms happen in the summer.

<u>Sleet</u> is smaller than hail. It begins to fall as rain. When it passes through a cold layer of air, it freezes. It lands as a bead of ice. Sleet falls in the winter.

Sometimes the air is warm but the ground is freezing. Then when it rains, the water freezes as it hits the ground. This coating of ice is called <u>glaze</u>.

Write the answers to the questions.

1. Where do hailstones freeze? <u>Hailstones freeze within a thundercloud.</u>

2. When do hailstorms happen? <u>Hailstorms happen in the summer.</u>

3. When does sleet freeze? <u>It freezes when it passes through a cold layer of air.</u>

4. When do you see sleet? <u>I see sleet in the winter.</u>

Let's Make a Book!

Look in books for pictures of thunderclouds. Read more about these summer storms. Draw a picture of a hailstorm for your book.

Page 32

Answer Key

Page 33

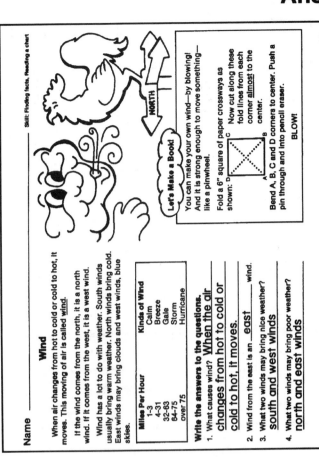

Name _____

Wind

When air changes from hot to cold or cold to hot, it moves. This moving of air is called wind.

If the wind comes from the north, it is a north wind. If it comes from the west, it is a west wind.

Wind has a lot to do with weather. North winds bring cold. South winds usually bring warm weather. North winds bring clouds and west winds, blue skies.

Miles Per Hour	Kinds of Wind
1-3	Calm
4-31	Breeze
32-63	Gale
64-75	Storm
over 75	Hurricane

Write the answers to the questions.

1. What causes wind? __When the air changes from hot to cold or cold to hot, it moves.__

2. Wind from the east is an __east__ wind.

3. What two winds may bring nice weather? __south and west winds__

4. What two winds may bring poor weather? __north and east winds__

Let's Make a Book!

You can make your own wind—by blowing! And it is strong enough to move something—like a pinwheel.

Fold a 6" square of paper crossways as shown:

Now cut along these fold lines from each corner almost to the center. Push a pin through and into pencil eraser.

Bend A, B, C and D corners to center.

BLOW!

Page 34

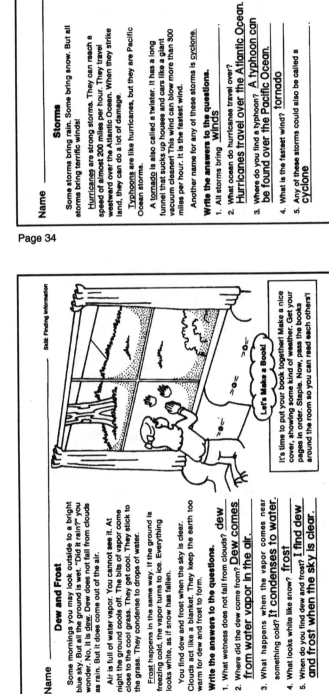

Name _____

Storms

Some storms bring rain. Some bring snow. But all storms bring terrific winds!

Hurricanes are strong storms. They can reach a speed of almost 200 miles per hour. They travel westward over the Atlantic Ocean. When they strike land, they can do a lot of damage.

Typhoons are like hurricanes, but they are Pacific Ocean storms.

A tornado is also called a twister. It has a long funnel that sucks up houses and cars like a giant vacuum cleaner! This wind can blow more than 300 miles per hour. It is the fastest wind.

Another name for any of these storms is cyclone.

Write the answers to the questions.

1. All storms bring __winds__

2. What ocean do hurricanes travel over? __Hurricanes travel over the Atlantic Ocean.__

3. Where do you find a typhoon? __A typhoon can be found over the Pacific Ocean.__

4. What is the fastest wind? __tornado__

5. Any of these storms could also be called a __cyclone__

Let's Make a Book!

Choose a story starter to write an adventure story:

1. All morning they've been saying that a hurricane was on its way. My neighbors are leaving to find a safe place to wait. But I can't leave because . . .

2. I lived in a small town in Texas. We raised cotton. Last week something awful happened: a tornado hit! It began on Tuesday. We were all watching those clouds. . . .

Page 35

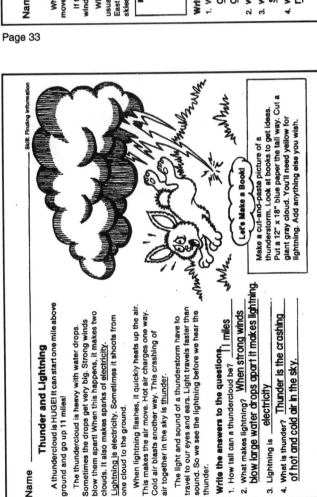

Name _____

Thunder and Lightning

A thundercloud is HUGE! It can start one mile above ground and go up 11 miles!

The thundercloud is heavy with water drops. Sometimes the drops get very big. Strong winds blow them apart. When this happens, it makes two clouds. It also makes sparks of electricity. Lightning is electricity. Sometimes it shoots from one cloud to the ground.

When lightning flashes, it quickly heats up the air. This makes the air move. Hot air charges one way. Cold air blasts another way. This crashing of air together in the sky is thunder.

The light and sound of a thunderstorm have to travel to our eyes and ears. Light travels faster than sound. So we see the lightning before we hear the thunder.

Write the answers to the questions.

1. How tall can a thundercloud be? __11 miles__

2. What makes lightning? __When strong winds blow large water drops apart it makes lightning.__

3. Lightning is __electricity__

4. What is thunder? __Thunder is the crashing of hot and cold air in the sky.__

Let's Make a Book!

Make a cut-and-paste picture of a thunderstorm. Look at books to get ideas. Put a 12" x 18" blue paper the tall way. Cut a giant gray cloud. You'll need yellow for lightning. Add anything else you wish.

Page 36

Name _____

Dew and Frost

Some mornings you may look outside to a bright blue sky. But all the ground is wet. "Did it rain?" you wonder. No, it is dew. Dew does not fall from clouds as rain. But it does come out of the air.

Air is full of water vapor. You cannot see it. At night the ground cools off. The bits of vapor come close to the cool grass. They get cool. They stick to the grass. They condense to drops of water.

Frost happens in the same way. If the ground is freezing cold, the vapor turns to ice. Everything looks white, as if snow has fallen.

You find dew and frost when the sky is clear. Clouds act like a blanket. They keep the earth too warm for dew and frost to form.

Write the answers to the questions.

1. What wetness does not fall from clouds? __dew__

2. Where did the dew come from? __Dew comes from water vapor in the air.__

3. What happens when the vapor comes near something cold? __It condenses to water.__

4. What looks white like snow? __frost__

5. When do you find dew and frost? __I find dew and frost when the sky is clear.__

Let's Make a Book!

It's time to put your book together! Make a nice cover, showing some kind of weather. Get your pages in order. Staple. Now, pass the books around the room so you can read each others'!

Answer Key

Page 37

Name _____ *Skill: Writing definitions*

What's in Our Solar System?

An *astronomer*, or scientist who studies the universe, might make this list if you asked her what is in our solar system.

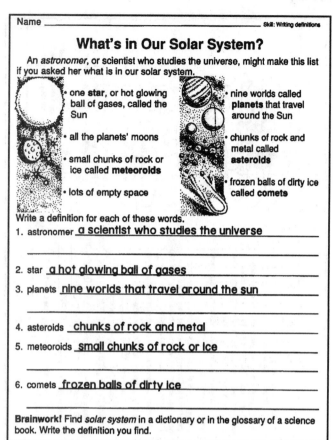

- one **star**, or hot glowing ball of gases, called the Sun
- all the planets' moons
- small chunks of rock or ice called **meteoroids**
- lots of empty space
- nine worlds called **planets** that travel around the Sun
- chunks of rock and metal called **asteroids**
- frozen balls of dirty ice called **comets**

Write a definition for each of these words.

1. astronomer _a scientist who studies the universe_

2. star _a hot glowing ball of gases_

3. planets _nine worlds that travel around the sun_

4. asteroids _chunks of rock and metal_

5. meteoroids _small chunks of rock or ice_

6. comets _frozen balls of dirty ice_

Brainwork! Find *solar system* in a dictionary or in the glossary of a science book. Write the definition you find.

Page 37

Page 38

Name _____ *Skill: Locating information*

Our Sun

When you see the Sun shining during the day, you are seeing a star. A star is a huge glowing ball of gases. The Sun is the only star in our solar system. It looks much larger than the stars we see at night because it is closer to us than the others. Even so, the Sun is 93 million miles from Earth.

Our Sun is really only a medium-size star. Some other stars in the universe are much bigger, and many stars are much smaller. The Sun is a yellow star. Hotter stars are blue and cooler stars are red.

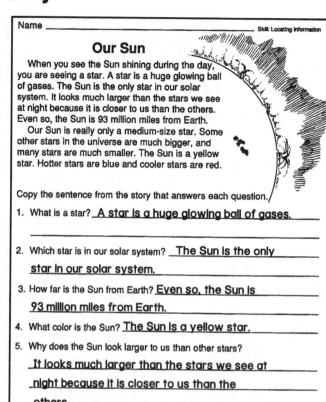

Copy the sentence from the story that answers each question.

1. What is a star? _A star is a huge glowing ball of gases._

2. Which star is in our solar system? _The Sun is the only star in our solar system._

3. How far is the Sun from Earth? _Even so, the Sun is 93 million miles from Earth._

4. What color is the Sun? _The Sun is a yellow star._

5. Why does the Sun look larger to us than other stars? _It looks much larger than the stars we see at night because it is closer to us than the others._

Brainwork! The Sun's light and heat help Earth's plants and animals to grow. Draw a picture to show this.

Page 38

Page 39

Name _____ *Skill: Scientific vocabulary*

The Planets Are Moving!

Each of the planets in our solar system **revolves**, or travels, around the Sun. The **planets** circle the Sun along paths called **orbits**. Because the planets are at different distances from the Sun, each one takes a different length of time to revolve once.

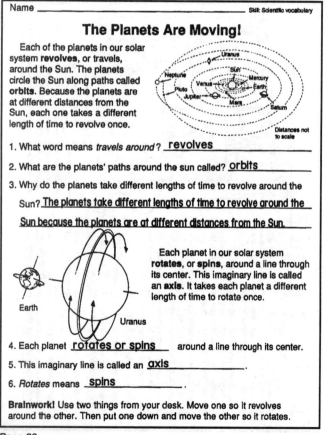

Distances not to scale

1. What word means *travels around*? _revolves_

2. What are the planets' paths around the sun called? _orbits_

3. Why do the planets take different lengths of time to revolve around the Sun? _The planets take different lengths of time to revolve around the Sun because the planets are at different distances from the Sun._

Each planet in our solar system **rotates**, or **spins**, around a line through its center. This imaginary line is called an **axis**. It takes each planet a different length of time to rotate once.

Earth

Uranus

4. Each planet _rotates or spins_ around a line through its center.

5. This imaginary line is called an _axis_.

6. *Rotates* means _spins_.

Brainwork! Use two things from your desk. Move one so it revolves around the other. Then put one down and move the other so it rotates.

Page 39

Page 40

Name _____ *Skill: Unscrambling words*

Solar System Scramble

Unscramble the name of each numbered object below. Write the name on the correct line below.

Word Box
Neptune
asteroids
Mars
Earth
Jupiter
Sun
Saturn
Uranus
Pluto
Venus
Mercury

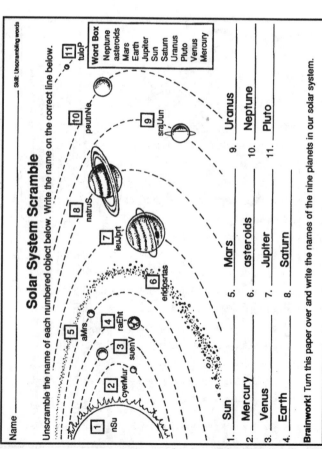

1. _Sun_
2. _Mercury_
3. _Venus_
4. _Earth_
5. _Mars_
6. _asteroids_
7. _Jupiter_
8. _Saturn_
9. _Uranus_
10. _Neptune_
11. _Pluto_

Brainwork! Turn this paper over and write the names of the nine planets in our solar system.

Page 40

FS-32049 Science

Answer Key

A Strip of Space

Follow these directions to compare the positions of the planets from the Sun.   *Strip is completed as directed.*

1. Color:
   - the Sun yellow
   - Mercury brown
   - Venus yellow
   - Earth green
   - Mars red
   - Jupiter orange
   - Saturn yellow
   - Uranus and Neptune blue
   - Pluto purple

2. Cut out the four strips.

3. Glue:
   - strip 2 to the right end of strip 1
   - strip 3 to the right end of strip 2
   - strip 4 to the right end of strip 3

(Distances are to approximate scale.)

Sun Venus Mars
Mercury Earth
Jupiter
Saturn   1. glue

2. glue   Uranus

3. glue   Neptune

Pluto   4.

Page 41

Mercury—Closest to the Sun

Mercury is the planet closest to the Sun. That is why Mercury travels around the Sun faster than any other planet. It takes Mercury 88 days to revolve once around the Sun.

Little was known about Mercury before 1974. Scientists have a hard time studying Mercury with telescopes because of the Sun's great light. In 1974 and 1975 an unmanned spacecraft named *Mariner X* flew by Mercury three times and sent scientists new information about the planet.

The surface of Mercury is much like the moon's surface. It has high cliffs and deep craters, or holes. Mercury has almost no atmosphere, or gases surrounding it. Temperatures on the planet range from 950° F to –210° F! Mercury has no moons.

Write each answer in a sentence.

1. Which planet is closest to the Sun? **Mercury is the planet closest to the Sun.**

2. How long does it take Mercury to revolve around the Sun? **It takes Mercury 88 days to revolve once around the Sun.**

3. Why do scientists have a hard time studying Mercury with telescopes? **Scientists have a hard time studying Mercury because of the Sun's great light.**

4. What did Mariner X do? **Mariner X flew by Mercury three times and sent scientists new information.**

5. Describe Mercury's surface. **It is like the moon's surface. It has high cliffs and deep craters.**

Brainwork! Make a list of three interesting facts about Mercury.

Page 42

Venus—Earth's Twin

Use the words in the Word Bank to complete the story.

Word Bank			
light	against	lightning	size
closest	higher	atmosphere	melt

Venus has been called Earth's twin because it is about the same **size** (1) as Earth. Venus is the second planet from the Sun and is the planet **closest** (2) to Earth. Venus was also the first planet to be studied by spacecraft. Venus has no moon.

Venus has an interesting **atmosphere** (3), or blanket of gases around it. It reflects, or bounces off, so much of the Sun's **light** (4) that Venus is easier to see than any other planet. The atmosphere also lets some sunlight in and traps heat **against** (5) the planet's surface. Therefore, temperatures on Venus are high enough to **melt** (6) some metals. Clouds move at high speeds in Venus's atmosphere, and bolts of **lightning** (7) streak across its sky.

Venus has volcanoes on its surface and a mountain **higher** (8) than the highest on Earth. There is no liquid water on Venus. Earth's plants and animals could not live on Venus.

Brainwork! Think of another nickname for Venus. Write to tell why it is a good nickname.

Page 43

Our Home Planet

Use the words from the Word Bank to complete the story.

Word Bank					
	closer	soil	Sun		
distance	reaches	main	planet	Earth	liquid

The third planet from the **Sun** (1) is our home planet Earth. Earth has something no other **planet** (2) is known to have—living things.

Earth is at the right **distance** (3) from the Sun to have the liquid water necessary to support life. Mercury and Venus are too hot because they are **closer** (4) to the Sun. The other planets are too far from the Sun to have **liquid** (5) water. Not much heat or light **reaches** (6) them, so the water would be in the form of ice.

Earth has a lot of water. Most living things need water. Water helps to control the earth's weather and climate. Water also breaks rocks into **soil** (7) which plants need to grow.

Earth is surrounded by a blanket of air called the atmosphere. Oxygen is one of the **main** (8) gases in the atmosphere. Most animals breathe oxygen.

Earth (9) is a special planet!

Brainwork! Design a poster showing why Earth is a good planet for living things.

Page 44

115

Answer Key

We See Our Moon

Earth has one moon. It is the moon that we see in the sky. The moon is Earth's partner in space. It makes a path around, or **orbits**, Earth. It also orbits the Sun along with the earth.

The moon looks large because it is closer to Earth than the Sun or planets. Four moons would stretch across the **diameter**, or widest part of the earth.

In 1969 **astronaut** Neil Armstrong took the first steps on the moon. Scientists have studied rocks brought back from the moon.

The surface of the moon has many deep holes called **craters**. It has flat areas called **maria**. The moon also has rocky mountain areas called **highlands**. There is no air, wind, or water on the moon. No life exists there.

Write the word in dark print from the story that matches each definition.

1. deep holes in the moon's surface	2. to make a path around	3. flat land on the moon
craters	orbits	maria

4. the widest part of the earth	5. areas with rocky mountains	6. a person who travels in space
diameter	highlands	astronaut

Write two sentences about the moon using two of the words in dark print.

1. *Sentences will vary.* _____

_____

2. _____

_____

Brainwork! Would you like to visit the moon? Write to explain your answer.

Page 45

Mars—The Red Planet

Mars, the fourth planet from the Sun, is half the size of Earth. Mars has two moons. It has been called the Red Planet because of its red color. Parts of this planet's surface are covered with sand dunes and dry reddish deserts. Other areas look like dried up riverbeds. Some scientists believe water may once have flowed on Mars. Mars also has two polar caps made up of frozen water and dry ice. Pink, blue, and white clouds move through the Red Planet's sky.

For a long time some people thought there might be life on Mars. When two U.S. spacecraft landed on the planet in 1976, they sent back photographs of Mars and did experiments to find out if life exists there. Scientists now believe that Mars does not have plant or animal life like that on Earth.

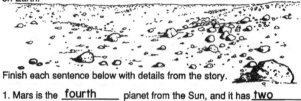

Finish each sentence below with details from the story.

1. Mars is the __fourth__ planet from the Sun, and it has __two__ moons.

2. Mars is nicknamed the __Red Planet__.

3. Two U.S. spacecraft landed on Mars in __1976__, sent back photographs, and did __experiments__.

4. Mars has dry reddish __deserts__ and what look like dried up __riverbeds__.

5. Mars has two __polar caps__ made of frozen water and dry ice.

Brainwork! Draw and color a picture that shows your idea of the Red Planet's landscape.

Page 46

Jumbo Jupiter

Jupiter is the largest of the nine planets. It is more than 11 times larger than Earth.

Jupiter is the fifth planet from the Sun, and it travels once around the Sun every 12 years. This jumbo planet rotates in just ten hours—faster than any other planet!

Thick clouds surround Jupiter. Most scientists believe that the belts of color in Jupiter's atmosphere are caused by different gases. The planet is a giant ball of liquids and gases with, perhaps, a small rocky core. Its famous Great Red Spot is a huge storm of swirling gases. Lightning streaks across Jupiter's sky. Jupiter has a thin dust ring around its middle and 16 known moons.

Jupiter's Great Red Spot

Write true or false.

false	1. Jupiter is the smallest planet in our solar system.
false	2. Earth is larger than Jupiter.
true	3. It takes 12 years for Jupiter to travel around the Sun.
true	4. Jupiter rotates faster than any other planet.
true	5. Jupiter's Great Red Spot is a huge storm of swirling gases.
false	6. Jupiter has a thick ice ring around its middle.
true	7. Jupiter has more than ten moons.
false	8. Jupiter is the sixth planet from the sun.

Brainwork! Write one true and one false statement about Jupiter. Have a friend tell which is true and which is false.

Page 47

Stunning Saturn

Saturn is the sixth planet from the Sun. Saturn is best known for the beautiful rings around its middle. The rings are thin and flat and made of pieces of rock and ice. They stretch more than 100,000 miles across!

Some scientists believe the rings are made of particles left over from the time when Saturn first became a planet. Others believe the rings are made of pieces of a moon that was torn apart when it came too close to Saturn.

Saturn is the second largest planet. Since Saturn is more than nine times farther than Earth is from the Sun, it is much colder than Earth. The planet is a giant ball of spinning gases. Saturn has at least 20 moons.

Write each answer in a sentence.

1. For what is Saturn best known? __Saturn is best known for the beautiful rings around its middle.__

2. What is one idea scientists have about how Saturn's rings were made? *Answers vary.* _____

_____

3. How does Saturn compare in size with the other planets? __Saturn is the second largest planet.__

4. Why is Saturn colder than Earth? __Saturn is more than nine times farther than Earth is from the Sun.__

5. How many moons does Saturn have? __Saturn has at least 20 moons.__

Brainwork! Write a poem about Saturn's beautiful rings.

Page 48

Answer Key

Name ______________________ Skill: Locating information

The Blue-green Giants

Uranus and Neptune are giant planets more than a billion miles from the Sun and Earth. They are about the same size. Each is more than $3\frac{1}{2}$ times larger than Earth. They look blue-green in photos because both have a gas called methane in their atmospheres. Uranus and Neptune are very cold planets where life probably doesn't exist.

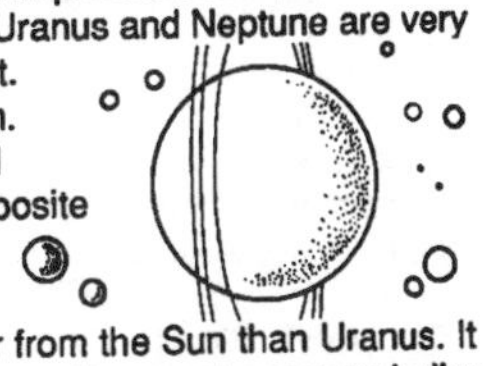

Uranus is the seventh planet from the Sun. It is known to have at least 15 moons and 11 thin rings. Uranus rotates in the direction opposite to that of Earth. It can be seen from Earth without a telescope.

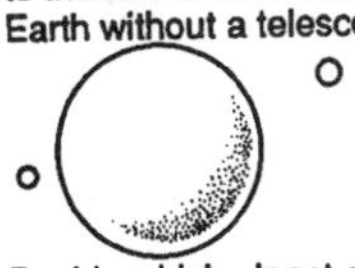

Neptune is farther from the Sun than Uranus. It has eight known moons. Some astronomers believe it may also have a ring. Neptune cannot be seen without a telescope.

Decide which planet or planets each fact describes. If it describes Uranus, write *Uranus*. If it describes Neptune, write *Neptune*. If it describes both Uranus and Neptune, write *both*.

1. rotates in the opposite direction **Uranus**
2. called a blue-green giant **both**
3. cannot be seen without a telescope **Neptune**
4. is more than a billion miles from Earth **both**
5. has methane in its atmosphere **both**
6. has at least 11 rings **Uranus**
7. can be seen without a telescope **Uranus**
8. has eight known moons **Neptune**

Brainwork! List three ways Uranus and Neptune are alike. List three ways they are different.

Page 49

Name ______________________ Skill: Unscrambling facts

Faraway Pluto

Pluto travels farther from the Sun than any other planet in our solar system. At its farthest point, it is more than four billion miles from Earth!

Pluto is also the smallest of the nine known planets. It is smaller than Earth's moon.

Scientists know very little about the planet Pluto because it is so far away. It is believed to be like a rocky snowball in space. Charon is Pluto's only moon. Scientists don't think any life exists on faraway Pluto.

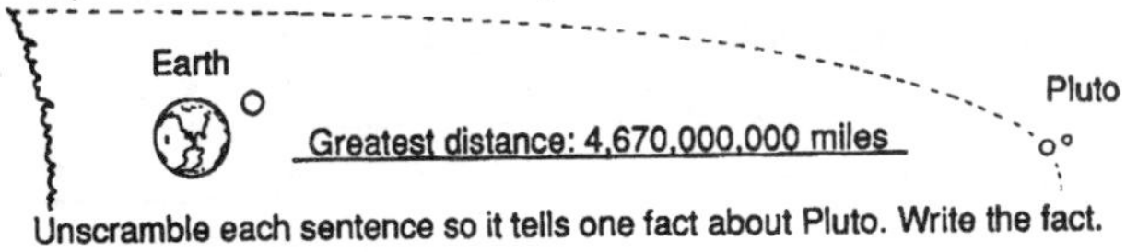

Unscramble each sentence so it tells one fact about Pluto. Write the fact.

1. farthest Sun Pluto travels from the
   Pluto travels farthest from the Sun.
2. has moon one Pluto
   Pluto has one moon.
3. planet smallest Pluto is the
   Pluto is the smallest planet.
4. travels billion more four than Earth from miles Pluto
   Pluto travels more than four billion miles from Earth.
5. Pluto's named is Charon moon
   Pluto's moon is named Charon.

Brainwork! Write two questions you would like to ask an astronomer about Pluto or its moon.

Page 50

Name ______________________ Skill: Using a chart and diagram

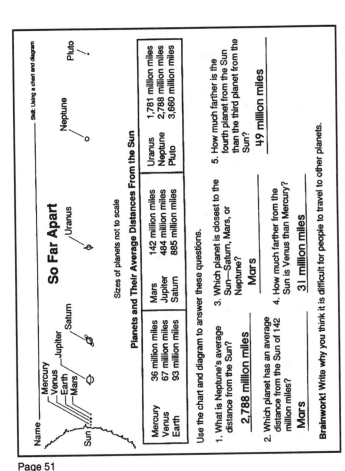

So Far Apart

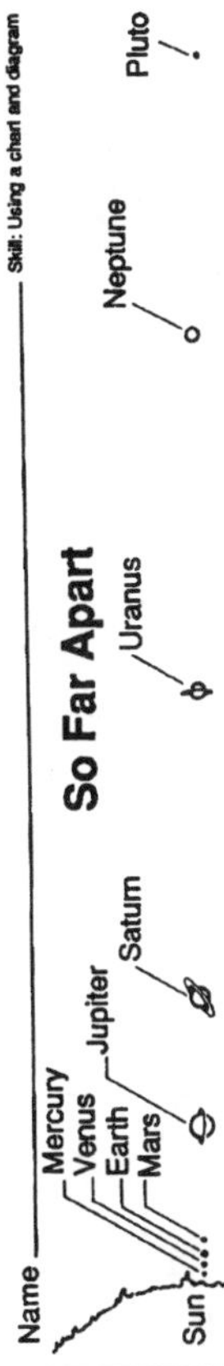

Sizes of planets not to scale

Planets and Their Average Distances From the Sun

Mercury	36 million miles	Mars	142 million miles	Uranus	1,781 million miles
Venus	67 million miles	Jupiter	484 million miles	Neptune	2,788 million miles
Earth	93 million miles	Saturn	885 million miles	Pluto	3,660 million miles

Use the chart and diagram to answer these questions.

1. What is Neptune's average distance from the Sun? **2,788 million miles**
2. Which planet has an average distance from the Sun of 142 million miles? **Mars**
3. Which planet is closest to the Sun—Saturn, Mars, or Neptune? **Mars**
4. How much farther from the Sun is Venus than Mercury? **31 million miles**
5. How much farther is the fourth planet from the Sun than the third planet from the Sun? **49 million miles**

Brainwork! Write why you think it is difficult for people to travel to other planets.

Page 51

Name ______________________ Skill: Using a chart and diagram

The Planets' Names

Match each symbol in the puzzle to a clue below. Write the planet's name across or down in capital letters.

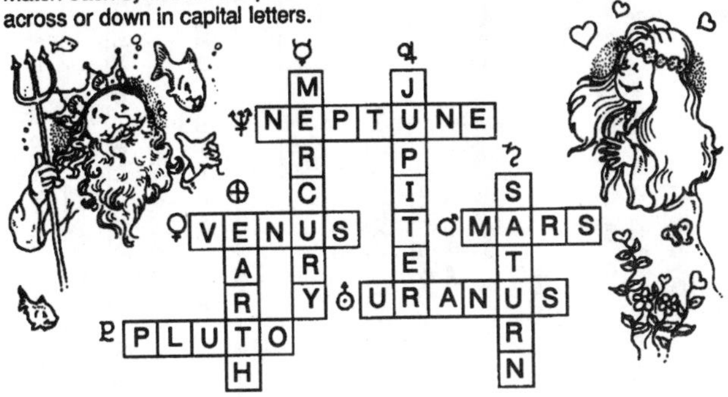

Across

♆ Neptune was named after the Roman god of the sea.
♀ Venus was named after the Roman goddess of love and beauty.
♂ Mars was named after the Roman god of war.
⛢ Uranus was named after the Greek god of the sky.
♇ Pluto was named after the Greek and Roman god of the lower world.

Down

☿ Mercury was named after the Roman messenger of the gods.
♃ Jupiter was named after the Roman king of the gods and ruler of the universe.
♄ Saturn was named after the Roman god of farming.
⊕ Earth was named after the Greek earth goddess.

Brainwork! Make a word search puzzle with the planets' names. Have a friend solve your puzzle.

Page 52

© Frank Schaffer Publications, Inc.

Answer Key

My Planet Report

Name _____ Skill: Gathering information

My Planet Report

Name of the planet _____

Named after _____ *Answers will vary on this page.*

Size of the planet _____

Average distance from the Sun _____

Time needed to revolve around the Sun _____

Time needed to rotate on its axis _____

Facts about the planet's surface _____

Facts about the planet's moon(s) _____

Other interesting facts _____

My information came from _____

A picture of my planet

My planet's symbol

Page 53

Interesting Moons

Name _____ Skill: Using a code

Interesting Moons

Use the code to discover the names of some moons in our solar system.

A	B	C	D	E	F	G	H	I	J	K	L	M
1	2	3	4	5	6	7	8	9	10	11	12	13

N	O	P	Q	R	S	T	U	V	W	X	Y	Z
14	15	16	17	18	19	20	21	22	23	24	25	26

A. Jupiter's moon named __I__ __O__ has at least eight active volcanoes.
    9 15

B. __P__ __H__ __O__ __B__ __O__ __S__ travels around Mars in $7\frac{1}{2}$ hours. No other
  16 8 15 2 15 19
moon travels so fast.

C. Jupiter also has the largest moon in the solar system. It is named
  __G__ __A__ __N__ __Y__ __M__ __E__ __D__ __E__ .
   7 1 14 25 13 5 4 5

D. __T__ __I__ __T__ __A__ __N__ is known to have a thick atmosphere. It is one of
  20 9 20 1 14
Saturn's moons.

E. Neptune's moon __T__ __R__ __I__ __T__ __O__ __N__ orbits the planet backwards.
       20 18 9 20 15 14

F. __D__ __E__ __I__ __M__ __O__ __S__ is the smallest Martian moon.
  4 5 9 13 15 19

G. __E__ __U__ __R__ __O__ __P__ __A__ is one of Jupiter's 16 moons.
  5 21 18 15 16 1

H. The first footsteps on another surface in space
were taken on Earth's __M__ __O__ __O__ __N__
              13 15 15 14

Brainwork! Which moon above would you most like to visit? Write a paragraph telling which moon you would choose and why.

Page 54

Beyond Our Solar System

Skill: Comprehension

Side View of the Milky Way

Our Solar System

Beyond Our Solar System

Astronomers know that much lies beyond our solar system. In fact, in the drawing on this page our solar system is just a tiny speck in a larger group of objects in space. This larger group is called the Milky Way galaxy. The Milky Way is made up of all the stars you can see in the night sky and many more beyond those. It also contains large clouds made of gas and dust. But that's not all! Beyond our Milky Way, astronomers have seen millions of other galaxies. Each of these has billions of stars. Astronomers call space and everything in it the universe.

1. What is the name of our galaxy? __Our galaxy is the Milky Way.__

2. What have astronomers seen beyond our galaxy? __Astronomers have seen millions of other galaxies.__

3. What is the universe? __The universe is space and everything in it.__

4. Which contains the largest group of objects—the solar system, the universe, or the Milky Way? __The universe contains the largest group of objects in space.__

5. What two kinds of objects does the Milky Way contain? __The Milky Way contains stars and large clouds made of gas and dust.__

Brainwork! Write a mini-book about the universe. Use the words *planet, solar system,* and *galaxy.*

Name _____

Page 55

A Review Riddle

Name _____ Skill: Vocabulary review

A Review Riddle

Find a word in the Word Bank that matches each clue below. Write the word on the blanks.

Word Bank
atmosphere   axis   revolve   planets
rings   star   orbit   astronomer
astronaut   rotate   craters

1. person who travels in space __a s t r o n a (u) t__
2. deep holes __(c) r a t e r s__
3. nine worlds __p (l) a n e t s__
4. to spin __(r) o t a t e__
5. to travel around __r e v o l v (e)__
6. scientist who studies the objects in space
  __a s t r o (n) o m e r__
7. imaginary line through the center of a planet __a x (i) s__
8. a planet's path around the sun __(o) r b i t__
9. ball of hot glowing gases __s t (a) r__
10. Saturn, Jupiter and Uranus have these __r i n g (s)__
11. a blanket of gases __a t m o s (p) h e r e__

Answer this riddle! Write the circled letters on the blanks below.

What is another name for our solar system?

__o u r__ __p l a c e__ __i n__ __s p a c e__
 8 1 4   11 3 9 2 5   7 6   10 11 9 2 5

Brainwork! Scramble the letters in each planet's name. Have a friend unscramble them.

Page 56

Answer Key

Unscrambling sentences

Sources of Heat

Find out about the many different ways we get heat. Look at these pictures. Then write a sentence about a source of heat by unscrambling each group of words. Remember to use capitals and periods!

Earth

Sun

1. earth   The   sun   the   heats
   The sun heats the earth.

2. gives   heat   us   A   fire
   A fire gives us heat.

3. hot   light   bulbs   makes   Electricity
   Electricity makes light bulbs hot.

4. heat   Gas   oil   and   homes
   Gas and oil heat homes.

5. two   together   heat   Rubbing   things   makes
   Rubbing two things together makes heat.

Try This! Heat is used for cooking. List three other uses for heat.

Page 57

Context clues

Fuels

Anything that is burned to produce heat is a fuel. People use fuels to heat homes, cook foods, and make hot water. Fuel also provides power for cars, trains, airplanes, and other kinds of transportation.

Long ago, people burned wood as fuel to make fire for heat and light. Later, people used oils from animal fat and plants to burn in lamps. The discovery of coal helped factories produce great amounts of power to make products. Today, petroleum, an oily liquid, is used to power most kinds of transportation. The natural gas that comes from wells drilled deep in the earth heats many homes.

USERS OF FUELS

Complete the sentences by filling in the missing letters.

1. _Fue l_ is anything that is burned to produce heat.
2. Wood and oi _l_ are fuels.
3. Long ago, people used wood to make _f i r e_.
4. People use fuels to _h e a t_ homes and _c oo k_ foods.
5. _C oa l_ is used in many factories.
6. _Pet r ol eu m_ is used to power cars, trains, and airplanes.
7. Many homes are heated by _n a t u r a l_ _g a s_.

Try This! Electricity is a type of fuel used to heat such things as stoves and dryers. List three things in your home that need electricity to produce heat.

Page 58

Locating information

Fahrenheit or Celsius?

A thermometer measures temperature.
Read about two kinds of scales used on thermometers.

Fahrenheit

The Fahrenheit scale is named after Gabriel Fahrenheit, a German scientist. On this scale, the freezing point of water is 32 degrees (32°F). This means that water turns from liquid to solid at 32°F. The boiling point of water is 212°F. A person's normal body temperature is 98.6°F. Most people in the United States use the Fahrenheit scale.

Celsius

The Celsius scale is named after Anders Celsius, a Swedish scientist. It is part of the metric system. Using this scale, the freezing point of water is 0 degrees (0°C) and the boiling point of water is 100°C. A person's normal body temperature is 37°C. Most countries around the world use the Celsius scale.

Read each phrase below. Write the name of the scale it describes.

1. water freezes at 0°
   Celsius
2. part of the metric system
   Celsius
3. water boils at 212°
   Fahrenheit
4. named after a German scientist
   Fahrenheit
5. used in most countries
   Celsius
6. water freezes at 32°
   Fahrenheit
7. named after a Swedish scientist
   Celsius
8. normal body temperature is 98.6°
   Fahrenheit

Try This! Do you think everyone in the world should use the same scale for measuring temperature? Write to explain your answer.

Page 59

Comprehension

Heat Travels

Heat travels from a warmer object to a cooler one. If you touch an ice cube, the heat moves from your finger to the ice. If you leave your finger on the ice, the ice cube will begin to melt. Suppose you touch a hot cup of tea. The heat from the cup will go to your fingers. OUCH! The heat from a hot pan will go to your hands and burn them if you don't use potholders to pick it up.

The movement of heat through solid materials is called **conduction**. Some materials are better conductors than others. That means they allow heat to pass through more quickly and easily. Aluminum and copper are good conductors. Wood and plastic are poor conductors.

Write the answers.

1. Does heat travel from a cold object to a hot one or from a hot object to a cold one? **Heat travels from a hot object to a cold one.**
2. What happens to an ice cube when you touch it with your finger? **The ice cube begins to melt.**
3. Why should you use potholders to pick up a hot pan? **I should use potholders to protect my hands from the heat.**
4. What is the movement of heat through solid materials called? **The movement of heat through solid materials is called conduction.**
5. Name two good conductors. **Aluminum and copper are good conductors.**
6. Name two poor conductors. **Wood and plastic are poor conductors.**

Try This! Design a poster to remind your family to use potholders when touching hot things. Display the poster in your kitchen.

Page 60

FS-32049 Science

Answer Key

Using an index

Finding Out About Heat

Use this index to write the correct page numbers on the blanks below.

Celsius, Anders, 53
Coal, how it is formed, 20–21
Fahrenheit, Gabriel, 52–53
Fire, 12–19
Fuels, 20–26
Heat, sources of, 8–20;
   how it travels, 38–40;
   experiments, 60–61

Natural gas, 25–26
Petroleum, where it is found, 22;
   petroleum products, 24–26
Sun, facts about, 8–11;
   protection from, 43–44
Thermometers, kinds of, 52–53;
   uses of, 54–55
Wood, 35–38

1. Heat experiments are discussed on pages __60–61__.
2. Information on natural gas is on pages __25–26__.
3. Pages __38–40__ tell how heat travels.
4. Hints about protecting yourself from sunburn are on pages __43–44__.
5. Information about Gabriel Fahrenheit is on pages __52–53__.
6. The last page on which you will find something about fire is page __19__.
7. Facts about kinds of thermometers are on pages __52–53__.
8. To find out the sun's temperature, look at pages __8–11__.
9. You will find out about Anders Celsius on page __53__.
10. Facts about wood are found on pages __35–38__.

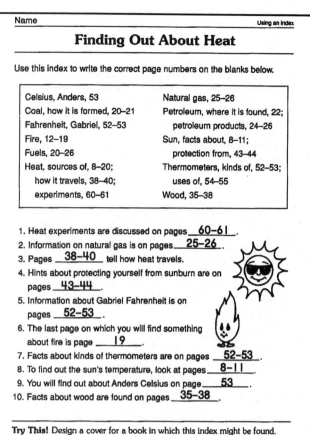

Try This! Design a cover for a book in which this index might be found.

Page 61

Review of heat

Can You Take the Heat?

Use the words in the puzzle to answer the questions. Then color each space in the puzzle with the color given beside the question.

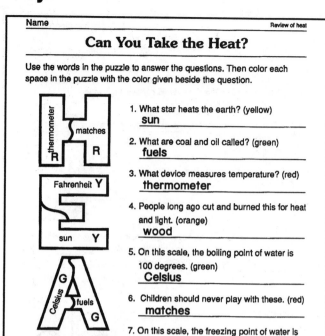

1. What star heats the earth? (yellow) __sun__

2. What are coal and oil called? (green) __fuels__

3. What device measures temperature? (red) __thermometer__

4. People long ago cut and burned this for heat and light. (orange) __wood__

5. On this scale, the boiling point of water is 100 degrees. (green) __Celsius__

6. Children should never play with these. (red) __matches__

7. On this scale, the freezing point of water is 32 degrees. (yellow) __Fahrenheit__

8. This makes a toaster hot. (orange) __electricity__

Try This! Make a poster showing five ways to cool off on a hot day.

Page 62

Classification

Sources of Light

Light can come from things found in nature. Most of our light comes from the sun. Light can also come from things made by people. For example, people make candles to use for light.

Some things that give light are pictured below. Decide whether they are found in nature or made by people. Write each one under the correct heading.

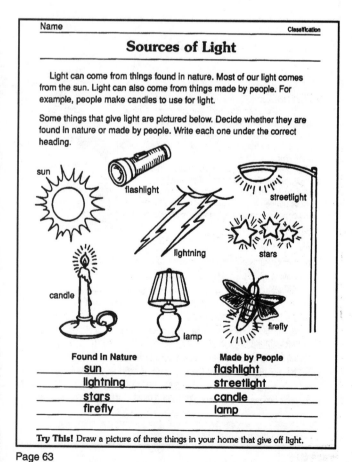

Found in Nature	Made by People
sun	flashlight
lightning	streetlight
stars	candle
firefly	lamp

Try This! Draw a picture of three things in your home that give off light.

Page 63

Context clues

Light and Sight

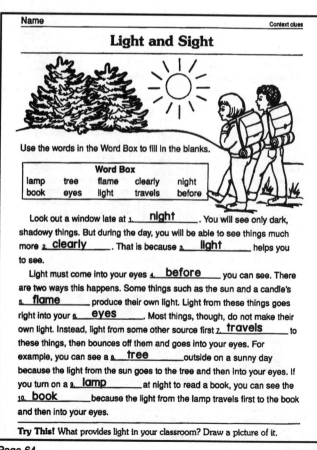

Use the words in the Word Box to fill in the blanks.

Word Box				
lamp	tree	flame	clearly	night
book	eyes	light	travels	before

Look out a window late at 1. __night__. You will see only dark, shadowy things. But during the day, you will be able to see things much more 2. __clearly__. That is because 3. __light__ helps you to see.

Light must come into your eyes 4. __before__ you can see. There are two ways this happens. Some things such as the sun and a candle's 5. __flame__ produce their own light. Light from these things goes right into your 6. __eyes__. Most things, though, do not make their own light. Instead, light from some other source first 7. __travels__ to these things, then bounces off them and goes into your eyes. For example, you can see a 8. __tree__ outside on a sunny day because the light from the sun goes to the tree and then into your eyes. If you turn on a 9. __lamp__ at night to read a book, you can see the 10. __book__ because the light from the lamp travels first to the book and then into your eyes.

Try This! What provides light in your classroom? Draw a picture of it.

Page 64

Answer Key

Crossword puzzle

Reflected Light

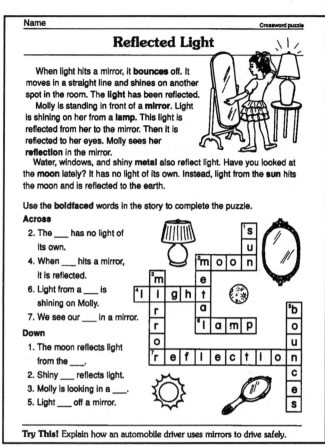

When light hits a mirror, it **bounces** off. It moves in a straight line and **shines** on another spot in the room. The **light** has been reflected.

Molly is standing in front of a **mirror**. Light is shining on her from a **lamp**. This light is reflected from her to the mirror. Then it is reflected to her eyes. Molly sees her **reflection** in the mirror.

Water, windows, and shiny **metal** also reflect light. Have you looked at the **moon** lately? It has no light of its own. Instead, light from the **sun** hits the moon and is reflected to the earth.

Use the boldfaced words in the story to complete the puzzle.

Across

2. The ___ has no light of its own.
4. When ___ hits a mirror, it is reflected.
6. Light from a ___ is shining on Molly.
7. We see our ___ in a mirror.

Down

1. The moon reflects light from the ___.
2. Shiny ___ reflects light.
3. Molly is looking in a ___.
5. Light ___ off a mirror.

Try This! Explain how an automobile driver uses mirrors to drive safely.

Page 65

Comprehension

A Band of Colors

Did you know that sunlight is really made up of a band of different colors? You can see these colors with the help of a prism. A prism is a transparent piece of glass that usually has three sides. Hold the prism in front of a window and let the sun shine through it. Turn the prism so that the light appears on a wall. As the light passes through the glass, it is separated into red, orange, yellow, green, blue, indigo (deep violet-blue), and violet. These are the same colors that appear in a rainbow or in a spray of water from a garden hose. That is because drops of water act like prisms, separating sunlight into different colors as the light passes through them.

Color the band of colors.

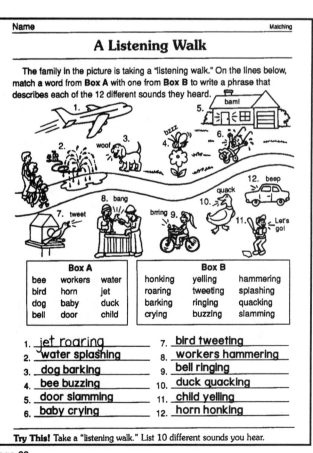

1. How many colors make up sunlight? __seven__
2. What is a prism? __A prism is a transparent piece of glass that usually has three sides.__
3. What happens to sunlight when it passes through a prism? __It is separated into seven different colors.__
4. What happens when sunlight passes through a spray of water? __The sunlight is separated into different colors. / The drops of water act like prisms.__

Try This! Design a bookmark that has all the colors of the rainbow.

Page 66

Word maze

The Speed of Light

Light travels about 186,000 miles a second. That is fast enough to go around the earth in the time it takes to blink an eye. It takes about eight minutes for light from the sun to reach the earth.

Scientists who study the stars are called **astronomers**. They call the distance light travels in one year a **light-year**. Light from a star named Alpha Centauri travels over four light-years to reach the earth. Light from Sirius, another star, travels eight and a half light-years to reach the earth!

Help each astronomer reach a star by following a path of words that form a sentence. Color the spaces as you go.

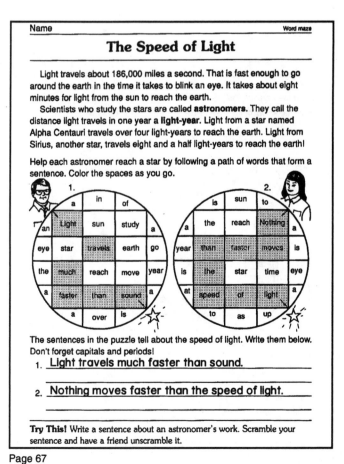

The sentences in the puzzle tell about the speed of light. Write them below. Don't forget capitals and periods!

1. __Light travels much faster than sound.__

2. __Nothing moves faster than the speed of light.__

Try This! Write a sentence about an astronomer's work. Scramble your sentence and have a friend unscramble it.

Page 67

Matching

A Listening Walk

The family in the picture is taking a "listening walk." On the lines below, match a word from **Box A** with one from **Box B** to write a phrase that describes each of the 12 different sounds they heard.

Box A			Box B		
bee	workers	water	honking	yelling	hammering
bird	horn	jet	roaring	tweeting	splashing
dog	baby	duck	barking	ringing	quacking
bell	door	child	crying	buzzing	slamming

1. __jet roaring__
2. __water splashing__
3. __dog barking__
4. __bee buzzing__
5. __door slamming__
6. __baby crying__
7. __bird tweeting__
8. __workers hammering__
9. __bell ringing__
10. __duck quacking__
11. __child yelling__
12. __horn honking__

Try This! Take a "listening walk." List 10 different sounds you hear.

Page 68

121

Answer Key

Vocabulary

Animal Sounds

Below each picture, write the sound the animal makes. Use the words in the box.

roar	moo
meow	oink
baa	woof
croak	tweet
growl	buzz
cluck	chirp
quack	

cat
1. m e o w

mosquito
2. b u z z

sheep
3. b a a

cricket
4. c h i r p

dog
5. w o o f

bear
6. g r o w l

pig
7. o i n k

lion
8. r o a r

duck
9. q u a c k

frog
10. c r o a k

chicken
11. c l u c k

cow
12. m o o

bird
13. t w e e t

Try This! List as many other animals and their sounds as you can in five minutes.

Page 69

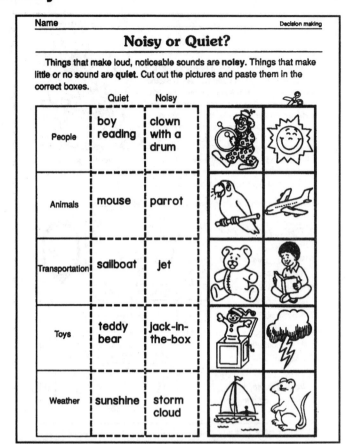

Decision making

Noisy or Quiet?

Things that make loud, noticeable sounds are **noisy**. Things that make little or no sound are **quiet**. Cut out the pictures and paste them in the correct boxes.

	Quiet	Noisy
People	boy reading	clown with a drum
Animals	mouse	parrot
Transportation	sailboat	jet
Toys	teddy bear	jack-in-the-box
Weather	sunshine	storm cloud

Page 70

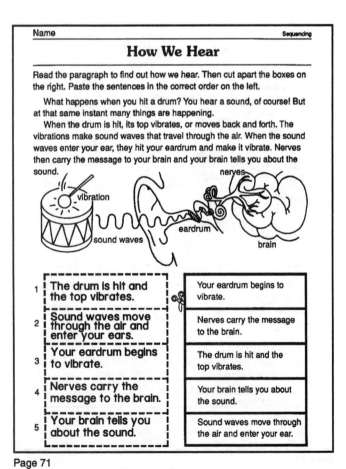

Sequencing

How We Hear

Read the paragraph to find out how we hear. Then cut apart the boxes on the right. Paste the sentences in the correct order on the left.

What happens when you hit a drum? You hear a sound, of course! But at that same instant many things are happening.

When the drum is hit, its top vibrates, or moves back and forth. The vibrations make sound waves that travel through the air. When the sound waves enter your ear, they hit your eardrum and make it vibrate. Nerves then carry the message to your brain and your brain tells you about the sound.

1	The drum is hit and the top vibrates.		Your eardrum begins to vibrate.
2	Sound waves move through the air and enter your ears.		Nerves carry the message to the brain.
3	Your eardrum begins to vibrate.		The drum is hit and the top vibrates.
4	Nerves carry the message to the brain.		Your brain tells you about the sound.
5	Your brain tells you about the sound.		Sound waves move through the air and enter your ear.

Page 71

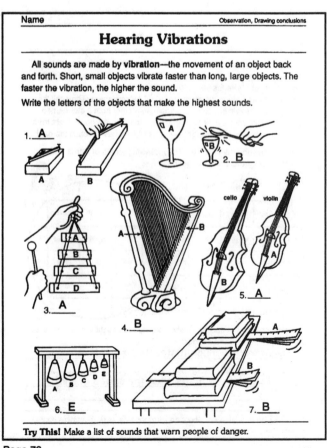

Observation, Drawing conclusions

Hearing Vibrations

All sounds are made by **vibration**—the movement of an object back and forth. Short, small objects vibrate faster than long, large objects. The faster the vibration, the higher the sound.

Write the letters of the objects that make the highest sounds.

1. A
2. B
3. A
4. B
5. A
6. E
7. B

Try This! Make a list of sounds that warn people of danger.

Page 72

---

122 FS-32049 Science

Answer Key

Sound Travels

Mr. Hunter told his class these facts about sound.

Sound waves are vibrations that move in all directions. They travel through gases (like air), liquids (like water), and solids (like glass). The closer you are to the source of the sound, the louder it seems.

The class did three experiments to learn how sound travels. On the lines write a conclusion they were able to draw from each experiment. Use the facts Mr. Hunter gave to help you.

1. Students stood in each corner of the classroom. Julio stood in the center and clapped his hands. All the students heard the clap at the same time.

Sound waves move in all directions.

2. The class stood on a sidewalk. The sound of a car became louder as it came closer. The sound became softer as the car got farther away from the students.

The closer you are to the source of the sound, the louder it seems.

3. Jim put his ear against the side of an aquarium. Kate tapped two rocks together underwater. Jim heard the taps through the glass and the water.

Sound travels through liquids and solids.

Try This! Long ago, American Indians put their ears to the ground to find out if horsemen were approaching before any horses could be seen. Explain how they were able to do this.

Page 73

Speak Up!

Put your fingers on your throat. Then read the next sentence out loud. You will feel the vocal cords inside your throat vibrating.

Down in the throat is the larynx, or voice box. To speak or sing, your brain sends messages telling the vocal cords to tighten. The air moving past the tightened cords causes them to vibrate. The vibrations make sounds. Working together, the tongue, shape of the lips, and vibration of the vocal cords let you make all the different sounds of the language you speak.

Write what each person below is saying. Use the sentences below.

I can feel my vocal cords vibrating in my throat.

My lips and tongue help me say my name—Lou!

My brain tells my vocal cords to tighten when I sing.

Two vocal cords stretch across the larynx.

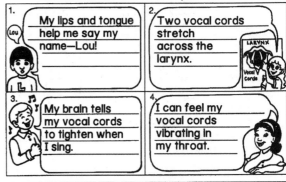

1. My lips and tongue help me say my name—Lou!

2. Two vocal cords stretch across the larynx.

3. My brain tells my vocal cords to tighten when I sing.

4. I can feel my vocal cords vibrating in my throat.

Try This! A ventriloquist talks without moving his lips. Make a bag puppet. Move the puppet's lips as you tell a joke like a ventriloquist.

Page 74

Echoes

Jumping into a swimming pool makes waves. The waves bounce off the sides of the pool and come back to the swimmer. Sound waves do the same thing. When they hit something flat and hard they bounce back. Sound waves that bounce back are called **echoes**.

Tara heard an echo on the playground yesterday. When she shouted to Dan, the sound waves of her voice traveled through the air to him. Some of the sound waves hit the school wall and bounced back. These waves came back as an echo.

Tara stepped back from the wall and shouted to Dan again. She discovered that as she moved farther away from the wall, the sound waves took longer to travel to the wall and return to her as an echo.

Use the shape-blocks to fill in the missing words.

1. Water waves and [sound] waves are alike because they both bounce back.

2. Sound waves bounce back when they hit something hard and [flat].

3. Sound waves from Tara's [voice] traveled through the air.

4. Some of the sound waves hit the school [wall] and bounced off.

5. Tara heard an [echo] after she shouted to Dan.

6. Tara stepped back and [shouted] to Dan again.

7. The sound waves took longer to come back as Tara moved farther [away] from the wall.

Try This! Bats send out high-pitched sounds as they fly at night. How do echoes warn them of danger and help them fly safely in the dark?

Page 75

A Sound Haiku Poem

Haiku poems are often about nature or the seasons. They have three lines containing a total of 17 syllables. The first line has 5 syllables, the second has 7 syllables, and the last has 5 syllables.

An example of a haiku poem:

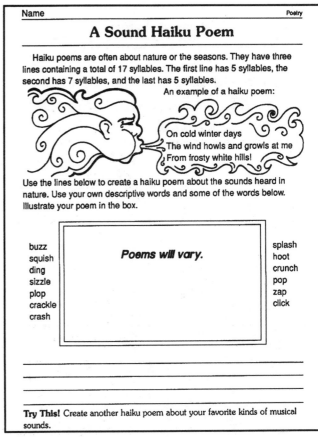

On cold winter days
The wind howls and growls at me
From frosty white hills!

Use the lines below to create a haiku poem about the sounds heard in nature. Use your own descriptive words and some of the words below. Illustrate your poem in the box.

buzz
squish
ding
sizzle
plop
crackle
crash

Poems will vary.

splash
hoot
crunch
pop
zap
click

Try This! Create another haiku poem about your favorite kinds of musical sounds.

Page 76

Answer Key

Name _____ Date _____

What Makes Me Grow?

I am growing bigger every day. I can tell! I have a coat that used to fit me. Now it is too small. I know I am growing. And this is how it happens:

Every day my bones get bigger. My skin gets bigger. Every part of me gets bigger. That's because my body keeps making more of itself!

All of me—my blood, my brain, my lungs—is made of something very special, called cells. A cell is very, very small. I can't see them, but they are alive! There are billions of them inside of me, too!

1. What are you doing every day?
I am gowing bigger.

2. How can you tell?
My clothes are too small.

3. How do you get bigger?
I get bigger because my body keeps making more of itself.

4. My whole body is made of:
cells

5. Why can't I see the cells?
The cells are very, very small.

6. How many are there?
There are billions of cells.

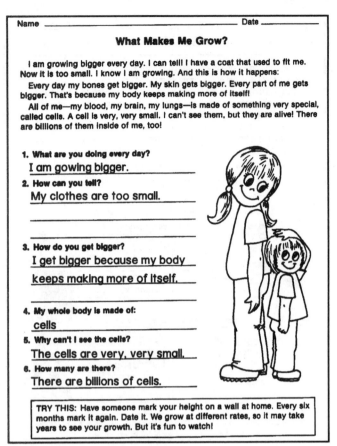

> **TRY THIS:** Have someone mark your height on a wall at home. Every six months mark it again. Date it. We grow at different rates, so it may take years to see your growth. But it's fun to watch!

Page 77

Name _____ Date _____

Billions of Cells!

Cells have many shapes. Some are round like a ball. Some are round and flat like a coin. Some are two feet long! Some cells live only a few days. Some live all my life.

Cells can be different in some ways. But most are alike in important ways. They are made the same on the inside. They can make more of themselves. **A cell can divide itself to become two cells!**

There are billions and billions of cells in me. And just think— when my life began, I was only one cell big!

1. What is one way cells can be different?
Answers vary.

2. Name two ways most cells are alike.
Cells are made the same on the inside. They can make more of themselves.

3. How do cells make more of themselves?
A cell can divide itself to become two cells.

4. How did you begin?
I began as one cell.

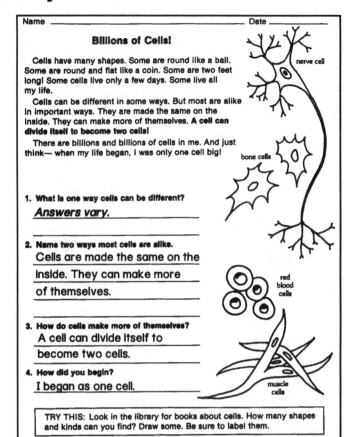

nerve cell

bone cells

red blood cells

muscle cells

> **TRY THIS:** Look in the library for books about cells. How many shapes and kinds can you find? Draw some. Be sure to label them.

Page 78

Name _____ Date _____

What Gives Me My Shape?

Sometimes at Halloween we scare people with play skeletons. But we shouldn't be afraid of skeletons. A skeleton cannot do anything by itself. It can only move inside of you and me.

I have to have a skeleton! If I did not, I would be floppy like a jellyfish! My skeleton gives me my shape. It also protects the important soft parts inside of me.

My skeleton is made of over 200 bones. They are locked together, but can still move. My bones are made of cells. They are alive and growing bigger every day!

1. Why shouldn't you be afraid of a skeleton?
A skeleton cannot do anything by itself.

2. When can skeletons move?
Skeletons can move only when they are inside of us.

3. About how many bones do you have?
I have over 200 bones.

4. Why do we have skeletons?
We have skeletons to give us shape and to protect our inner parts.

5. Why can your skeleton get bigger?
My skeleton is alive and growing.

6. What would you be like without a skeleton?
I would be floppy like a jellyfish.

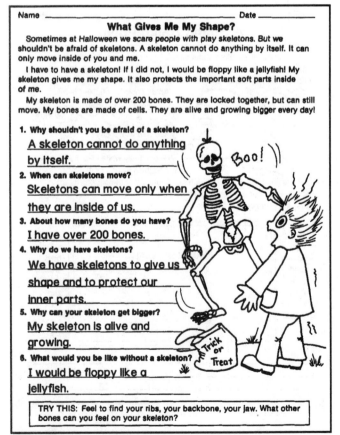

Boo!

Trick or Treat

> **TRY THIS:** Feel to find your ribs, your backbone, your jaw. What other bones can you feel on your skeleton?

Page 79

Name _____ Date _____

I can name these bones on my skeleton!

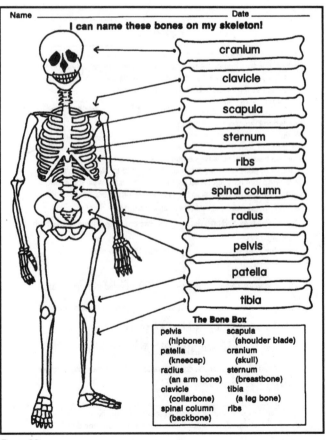

cranium

clavicle

scapula

sternum

ribs

spinal column

radius

pelvis

patella

tibia

The Bone Box

pelvis (hipbone)	scapula (shoulder blade)
patella (kneecap)	cranium (skull)
radius (an arm bone)	sternum (breastbone)
clavicle (collarbone)	tibia (a leg bone)
spinal column (backbone)	ribs

Page 80

FS-32049 Science

Answer Key

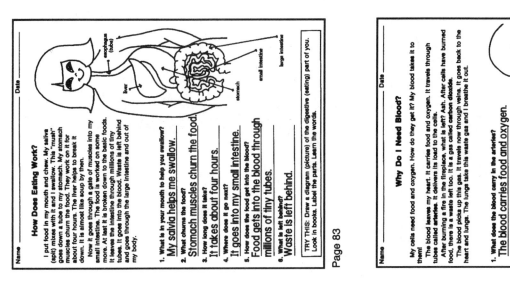

Page 83 — How Does Eating Work?

I put food in my mouth and chew. All living things must eat. My saliva (spit) mixes with it and I swallow. This "mush" goes down a tube to my stomach. My stomach muscles churn the food. They work on it for about four hours. The liver helps to break it down. It is almost like soup by then.

Now it goes through a gate of muscles into my small intestine. The food is worked on some more. At last it is broken down to the basic foods. It leaves the intestine through millions of tiny tubes. It goes into the blood. Waste is left behind and goes through the large intestine and out of my body.

1. What is in your mouth to help you swallow?
My saliva helps me swallow.

2. What churns the food?
Stomach muscles churn the food.

3. How long does it take?
It takes about four hours.

4. Where does it go next?
It goes into my small intestine.

5. How does the food get into the blood?
Food gets into the blood through millions of tiny tubes.

6. What is left behind?
Waste is left behind.

TRY THIS: Draw a diagram (picture) of the digestive (eating) part of you. Look in books. Label the parts. Learn the words.

Page 86 — Why Do I Need Blood?

My cells need food and oxygen. How do they get it? My blood takes it to them!

The blood leaves my heart. It carries food and oxygen. It travels through tubes called arteries. It delivers its load to the cells.

After burning a fire in the fireplace, what is left? Ash. After cells have burned food, there is a waste left too. It is a gas called carbon dioxide. The blood picks up this gas. It travels now through veins. It goes back to the heart and lungs. The lungs take this waste gas and I breathe it out.

1. What does the blood carry in the arteries?
The blood carries food and oxygen.

2. What is left after cells burn food?
Carbon dioxide is left.

3. What does the blood pick up?
The blood picks up carbon dioxide.

4. What does the blood flow through now?
The blood flows through veins.

5. Where does it go?
It goes back to the heart and lungs.

6. How do you get rid of the waste gas?
I breathe it out.

TRY THIS: Some of the veins and arteries are near your skin. Look at yourself carefully. Can you see some of these tubes? Look in a mirror. Look at your arms and hands.

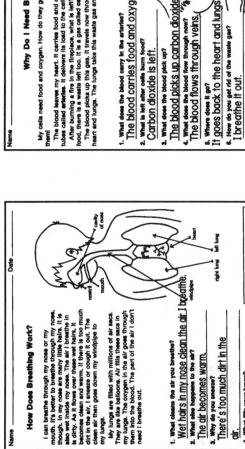

Page 82 — Why Do I Need to Eat?

My cells are alive, so they need food. All living things must eat. The food for my cells comes from what I eat. They cannot chew hamburgers and cake! They need the basic foods like sugar, fat, starch, and so on. All the food I eat is made of the basic foods.

My stomach breaks down the food I eat into a liquid. Then it becomes the basic food that cells need. My blood takes this basic food to my cells. The cells don't eat like I eat. They burn food. There is no flame, but it does make heat. That's why my body is warm. And that's what gives me energy!

1. What do all living things need?
All living things need food.

2. What food do cells need?
Cells need the basic foods like sugar, fat, and starch.

3. What does the stomach do?
The stomach breaks down the food I eat.

4. How does the food get to the cells?
Blood takes the food to the cells.

5. What do the cells do with it?
The cells burn it.

6. What two things does this burning give you?
This burning gives me warmth and energy.

TRY THIS: Find out about the basic foods. Use your library. Make a chart showing the food groups. Try to eat some of each group each day!

Page 85 — How Does Breathing Work?

I can breathe through my nose or my mouth. It's better to breathe through my nose, though. In my nose are many little hairs. It is also wet inside my nose. The air I breathe in is dirty. As it flows over these wet hairs, it becomes clean and warm. If there is too much dirt in the air, I sneeze or cough it out. The wet hairs clean the air then goes down my windpipe to my lungs.

My lungs are filled with millions of air sacs. They are like balloons. Air fills these sacs in my lungs. The oxygen in the air goes through them into the blood. The rest of the air I don't need I breathe out.

1. What cleans the air you breathe?
Wet hairs in my nose clean the air.

2. What also happens to the air?
The air becomes warm.

3. Why do you sneeze?
There's too much dirt in the air.

4. What fills your lungs?
My lungs are filled with millions of air sacs.

5. What goes through the sacs and into the blood?
Oxygen goes through them into the blood.

6. What do you do with the air you don't need?
I breathe it out.

TRY THIS: Draw a diagram of the breathing part of you. Label the parts. Learn the words.

Page 81 — What Makes Me Move?

I have a skeleton to give me my shape. But what makes my skeleton move? My muscles do! Almost all of me is covered with muscles. Muscles move my body.

Muscles move by pulling them. A muscle can pull because it can shorten itself. Muscles cannot push. It takes one pair of muscles to pull my arm up. It takes another pair to pull my arm down.

There are more than 500 muscles in my body. The more I use them, the stronger they get. That's why I should run and exercise a lot.

1. What moves your body?
Muscles move my body.

2. How do muscles work?
Muscles pull. / Muscles shorten themselves.

3. What can't muscles do?
Muscles cannot push.

4. How many muscles are needed to raise and lower your arm?
It takes two pairs of muscles.

5. How many muscles do you have?
I have more than 500 muscles.

6. Why is it important to get lots of exercise?
Exercise makes the muscles stronger.

TRY THIS: Stand up. Hold your hand on one of your calves. Now raise up on your tiptoes. Go up and down two or three times. You will feel your muscles working!

Page 84 — Why Do I Need to Breathe?

In the air is a gas called oxygen. Oxygen is needed when you build a fire. No burning can happen without oxygen. For my body's cells to burn food, they need oxygen. That is why I must breathe!

I breathe in. I take in air. It goes to my lungs. My lungs take the oxygen out of the air. This goes into my blood. The blood takes it to my cells. Now my cells can burn or "eat" the food.

1. Name a gas that is in the air.
Oxygen is in the air.

2. What do you need for burning?
Oxygen is needed for burning.

3. What do cells need before they can "eat"?
Cells need oxygen.

4. What do the lungs take out of the air?
Lungs take oxygen out of the air.

5. How does the oxygen get to the cells?
The blood takes it to the cells.

6. Now what can the cells do?
The cells can burn or "eat" the food.

TRY THIS: Find out all you can about oxygen. Also, find out why green plants are so important to us!

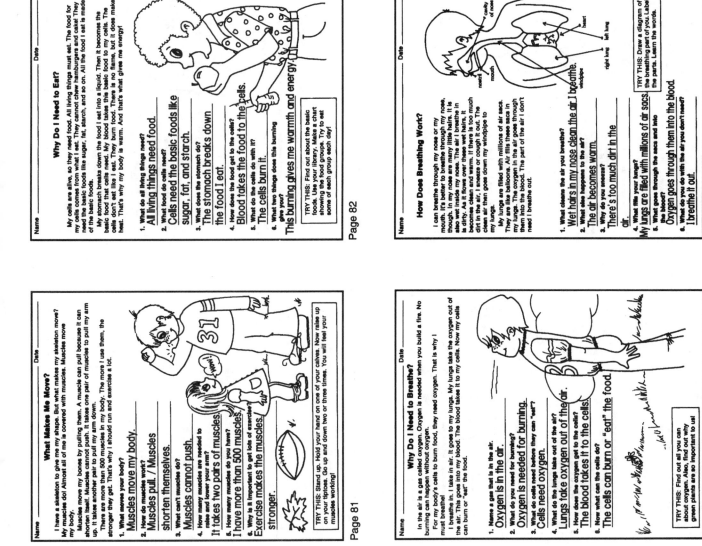

FS-32049 Science

Answer Key

© Frank Schaffer Publications, Inc.

FS-32049 Science

Name _____ **Date** _____

What Keeps My Blood Moving?

My blood moves because it is being pushed. It is pushed by a very strong pump: the heart.

My heart is not big. It is about the size of a fist. It weighs less than a pound. But it is strong! It is a bag of muscle. It has four "rooms." It has two pumps. This powerful "machine" keeps nine pints of blood flowing. It flows through more than 60,000 miles of tubes! The blood goes all through the body. My heart is just terrific!

1. How does your heart move your blood? **My heart pushes my blood.**
2. How big is your heart? **It is about the size of a fist.**
3. How much does it weigh? **It weighs less than a pound.**
4. Of what is it made? **It is made of muscle.**
5. How many pints of blood are in the body? **There are nine pints of blood.**
6. How many miles of tubes are there? **There are more than 60,000 miles of tubes.**

TRY THIS: Press your hand on the side of your neck, up near your jawbone. Feel the beat of your heart. Run fast. Feel again. See how your heart beats faster now? It is pushing the blood faster to feed the cells faster. This gives you quick energy.

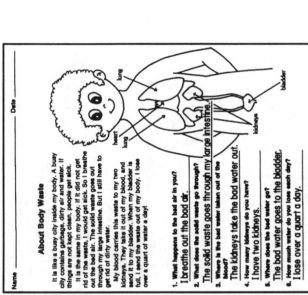

Page 87

Name _____ **Date** _____

About Body Waste

It is like a busy city inside my body. A busy city contains garbage, dirty air and water. If things are not kept clean, people get sick.

It is the same in my body. If it did not get rid of the waste, I would get sick. So I breathe out the bad air. The solid waste goes out through my large intestine. But I still have to get rid of dirty water.

My blood carries this waste to my two kidneys. They take it out of my blood, and send it to my bladder. When my bladder is full, I send the waste out of my body. I lose over a quart of water a day!

1. What happens to the bad air in your? **I breathe out the bad air.**
2. What does the solid waste go through? **The solid waste goes through my large intestine.**
3. Where is the bad water taken out of the blood? **The kidneys take the bad water out.**
4. How many kidneys do you have? **I have two kidneys.**
5. Where does the bad water go? **The bad water goes to the bladder.**
6. How much water do you lose each day? **I lose over a quart a day.**

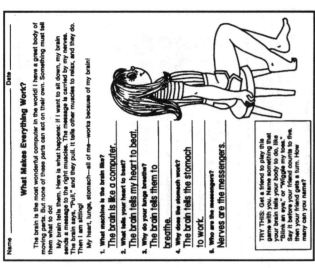

Page 88

Name _____ **Date** _____

What Makes Everything Work?

The brain is the most wonderful computer in the world! I have a great body of moving parts. But none of these parts can act on their own. Something must tell them what to do!

My brain tells them. Here is what happens: If I want to sit down, my brain sends a message to the right muscles. The message is carried by my nerves. The brain says, "Pull," and they pull. It tells other muscles to relax, and they do. Then I am sitting!

My heart, lungs, stomach—all of me—works because of my brain!

1. What machine is the brain like? **The brain is like a computer.**
2. What tells your heart to beat? **The brain tells my heart to beat.**
3. Why do your lungs breathe? **The brain tells them to breathe.**
4. Why does the stomach work? **The brain tells the stomach to work.**
5. Who are the messengers? **Nerves are the messengers.**

TRY THIS: Get a friend to play this game with you. Name something that your brain tells your body to do, like "Blink an eye," or "Wiggle my toe." Say it before your friend counts to five. How many can you name?

Page 89

Name _____ **Date** _____

How Do My Nerves Work?

My nerves are run by electricity! When the doorbell rings, the sound goes in my ears. An electrical charge goes along a path of my nerves to my brain. My brain tells me the doorbell is ringing. It sends the message to my muscles. They move me to the door.

I have billions of nerve cells. They start from all parts of my body. Most of them go up my spine. They go to the brain. Half of them send messages to my brain. The others take the message from the brain to the muscles and other parts of the body. Then they go into action.

1. What moves your nerve cells? **Electricity moves my nerve cells.**
2. Where does the message go? **The message goes to my brain.**
3. What do most of your nerves go through? **Most nerves go through my spine.**
4. How many nerve cells do you have? **I have billions of nerve cells.**
5. Where do they start? **They start from all parts of my body.**
6. Nerve cells take messages to my: **muscles or other parts of my body.**

TRY THIS: Get a set of Dominos. Stand them up tall, about an inch apart in a long line. Tap the first one. It will fall on the second one. That one will fall on the third one, and so on. This is a little like the way a message travels through your nerves.

Page 90

Name _____ **Date** _____

What Else Does My Brain Do?

I am glad my brain keeps my body working. But if that is all it did, I would be just an animal!

My brain has three parts. The smallest part, at the bottom, is the medulla. This part keeps my body living. It keeps the heart beating and the lungs breathing.

The part above it is the cerebellum. This part moves my muscles. It's also where I keep my balance.

The biggest part is the cortex. Here is where I think and decide, I remember and enjoy, I feel and understand.

1. What part of the brain keeps your body living? **The medulla keeps my body living.**
2. What part moves your muscles? **The cerebellum moves my muscles.**
3. Where does the thinking happen? **The cortex is where the thinking happens.**
4. What part keeps you breathing? **The medulla keeps me breathing.**
5. What part keeps your balance? **The cerebellum keeps my balance.**
6. What makes you enjoy things? **The cortex makes me enjoy things.**

$4 + 6 + 6 =$ hm-m-m-m!

TRY THIS: Draw a diagram of the brain. Label the parts. Find out more about the cortex. Each kind of nerve reports to its part of the brain (example: seeing and hearing). Mark those places.

Page 91

Name _____ **Date** _____ **Review**

My Brain

cortex
cerebellum
spinal cord
nerves
medulla
(blue)

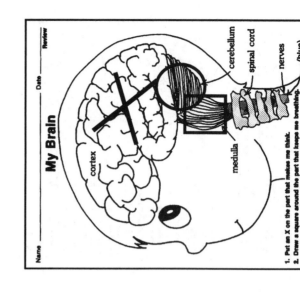

1. Put an X on the part that makes me think.
2. Draw a square around the part that keeps me breathing.
3. Draw a circle around the part that moves my muscles.
4. Color the parts where most of the nerves go through.
5. In blue, color the parts that are "messengers."

Page 92

Answer Key

The Mouse in the Jar — Biography

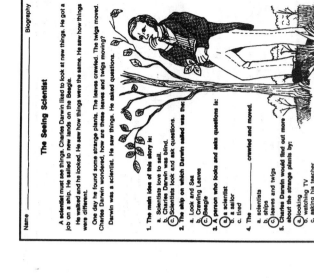

Joseph Priestley lit the candle and put the mouse into the jar. The candle went out. "Hmm," said Joseph. He put a mouse into the jar. The mouse looked sick. It could not breathe right. Hmm, thought Joseph. He opened the jar and let new air in for the mouse.

Joseph Priestley lit the candle and put the jar lid on. The candle went out again. This time he put a mint plant into the jar. He shut the lid tightly. Ten days later he put the mouse into the jar with the mint. The mouse ran around happily. "Aha!" cried Joseph. "The mint plant fixed the air. The mouse can breathe now."

Joseph had discovered something wonderful. He had found out that green plants make oxygen. Animals breathe oxygen from the air.

1. The main idea of this story is:
   a. Mice live in jars.
   b. **Green plants make oxygen.** *(circled)*
   c. Candles burn.

2. Animals get ____ from the air.
   a. water
   b. **oxygen** *(circled)*
   c. to take air in

3. To breathe means:
   a. to sing a lot
   b. to talk loudly
   c. **to take air in** *(circled)*

4. When the lid was on the jar, the candle:
   a. burned brightly
   b. stayed the same
   c. **went out** *(circled)*

5. Planting trees around your house:
   a. **helps make fresh air** *(circled)*
   b. takes air away
   c. brings mice

The Seeing Scientist — Biography

A scientist must see things. Charles Darwin liked to look at new things. He got a job on a ship. He sailed to new lands on the Beagle.

He walked and he looked. He saw how things were the same. He saw how things were different.

One day he found some strange plants. The leaves crawled. The twigs moved. Charles Darwin wondered, how are these leaves and twigs moving?

Darwin was a scientist. He saw things. He asked questions.

1. The main idea of this story is:
   a. Scientists love to sail.
   b. Charles Darwin was blind.
   c. **Scientists look and ask questions.** *(circled)*

2. The ship on which Darwin sailed was the:
   a. Look and Sea
   b. Crawling Leaves
   c. **Beagle** *(circled)*

3. A person who looks and asks questions is:
   a. **a scientist** *(circled)*
   b. a sailor
   c. tired

4. The ____ crawled and moved.
   a. scientists
   b. ships
   c. **leaves and twigs** *(circled)*

5. Charles Darwin would find out more about the strange plants by:
   a. **looking** *(circled)*
   b. watching TV
   c. asking his teacher

See How Much I Know!

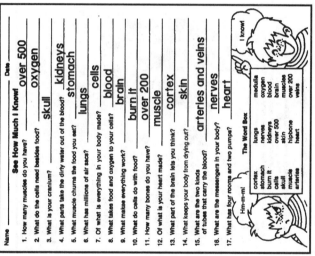

1. How many muscles do you have? **over 500**
2. What do the cells need besides food? **oxygen**
3. What is your cranium? **skull**
4. What parts take the dirty water out of the blood? **kidneys**
5. What muscle churns the food you eat? **stomach**
6. What has millions of air sacs? **lungs**
7. Of what is everything in your body made? **cells**
8. What takes food and oxygen to your cells? **blood**
9. What makes everything work? **brain**
10. What do cells do with food? **burn it**
11. How many bones do you have? **over 200**
12. Of what is your heart made? **muscle**
13. What part of the brain lets you think? **cortex**
14. What keeps your body from drying out? **skin**
15. What are the two kinds of tubes that carry the blood? **arteries and veins**
16. What are the messengers in your body? **nerves**
17. What has four rooms and two pumps? **heart**

The Word Box:

cortex	lungs	medulla
stomach	nerves	oxygen
burn it	kidneys	blood
cells	over 500	brain
skull	skin	muscles
muscle	hipbone	over 200
arteries	heart	veins

What About My Skin?

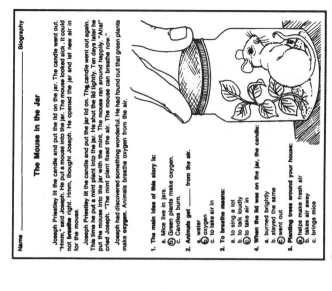

I can't see what's inside of me. And I'm glad about that! I'm covered with a perfect suit. The real name is skin.

I can never outgrow this suit-it grows with me! Being hot, cold, wet, or dry won't hurt it. It's perfect.

My skin protects me. It keeps germs out. Inside my body, it is very wet. My skin keeps my body from drying out. Sometimes my body gets too warm. Heat escapes through tiny holes called pores. My skin also sweats to cool me off.

What a super covering for my wonderful body!

1. How do you know skin is alive?
   It grows with me.

2. Tell one way skin protects you.
   It keeps germs out.

3. What is another way?
   It keeps the body from drying out.

4. What is one way to cool off?
   Heat escapes through pores.

5. Name another way.
   My skin sweats to cool me off.

TRY THIS: Get a paper towel. Put a blob of paint on it. Press your finger on it. Now press your finger on a piece of paper. This is a fingerprint. Have a friend do the same. See how it is different. No two people have the same!

Mother Goose — Biography

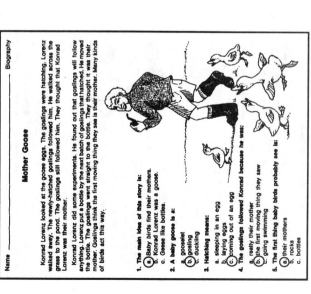

Konrad Lorenz looked at the goose eggs. The goslings were hatching. Lorenz walked away. The newly-hatched goslings followed him. He walked across the grass to the pond. The goslings still followed him. They thought that Konrad Lorenz was their mother.

Konrad Lorenz did some experiments. He found out that goslings will follow anything. Lorenz put a bottle by the next batch of goslings that hatched. He moved the bottle. The goslings went straight to the bottle. They thought it was their mother. Goslings think the first moving thing they see is their mother. Many kinds of birds act this way.

1. The main idea of this story is:
   a. **Baby birds find their mothers.** *(circled)*
   b. Konrad Lorenz was a goose.
   c. Geese like bottles.

2. A baby goose is a:
   a. gosset
   b. **gosling** *(circled)*
   c. duckling

3. Hatching means:
   a. sleeping in an egg
   b. laying eggs
   c. **coming out of an egg** *(circled)*

4. The goslings followed Konrad because he was:
   a. really their mother
   b. **the first moving thing they saw** *(circled)*
   c. going swimming

5. The first thing baby birds probably see is:
   a. their mothers
   b. rocks
   c. bottles

Blindfolds on Bats? — Biography

Bats come out at night. They fly around in the dark. They hunt for insects to eat. Bats' eyes are very little. Their ears are big.

Donald Griffin learned that bats do not use their eyes to find food. He put blindfolds on bats. He threw insects up into the air. His bats could still catch the insects.

Donald learned that bats squeak as they fly. The "squeak" sound hits the insects. The sound bounces back. The bouncing sound is an echo. The bat has big ears. It hears the echo and finds the insect.

1. The main idea of this story is:
   a. Bats use their eyes to hunt.
   b. **Bats use their ears to hunt.** *(circled)*
   c. Bats have little ears.

2. Donald Griffin kept bats because:
   a. **He wanted to learn about bats.** *(circled)*
   b. It was Halloween.
   c. Bats make good pets.

3. An echo is:
   a. a person yelling
   b. a loud noise
   c. **a sound that bounces back** *(circled)*

4. Donald Griffin found that bats:
   a. **do not use their eyes to find food** *(circled)*
   b. make no sounds
   c. eat rice

5. A bat could not find food if:
   a. **it could make no sound.** *(circled)*
   b. it was too dark.
   c. the moon was out.

Page 101 — Green Plants and Oxygen (Experiment)

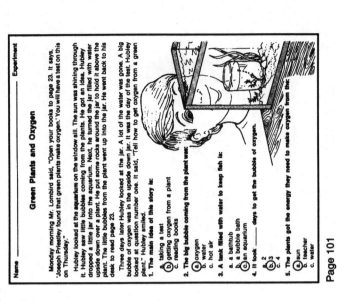

Monday morning Mr. Lombird said, "Open your books to page 23. It says, 'Joseph Priestley found that green plants make oxygen.' You will have a test on this on Thursday."

Hubley looked at the aquarium on the window sill. The sun was shining through it. Hubley saw little bubbles coming from the plants. He got an idea. Hubley dropped a little jar into the jar into the aquarium. Next, he turned the jar filled with water upside down over a plant. He put some rocks around the jar to hold it above the plant. The little bubbles from the plant went up into the jar. He went back to his desk to read page 23.

Three days later Hubley looked at the jar. A lot of the water was gone. A big bubble of oxygen was in the upside down jar. It was the day of the test. Hubley looked at question number one. It said, "Tell how to get oxygen from a green plant." Hubley smiled.

1. The main idea of this story is:
   a. taking a test
   (b) getting oxygen from a plant
   c. reading books

2. The big bubble coming from the plant was:
   (a) oxygen
   b. water
   c. hot air

3. A tank filled with water to keep fish is:
   a. a bathtub
   b. a bubble bath
   (c) an aquarium

4. It took ___ days to get the bubble of oxygen:
   a. 2
   (b) 3
   c. 4

5. The plants got the energy they need to make oxygen from the:
   (a) sun
   b. teacher
   c. water

Page 104 — Review

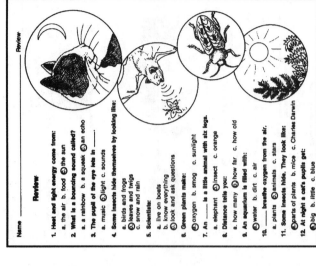

1. Heat and light energy come from:
   a. the air   b. food   (c) the sun

2. What is a bouncing sound called?
   a. a rainbow   b. a squeak   (c) an echo

3. The pupil of the eye lets in:
   a. music   (b) light   c. sounds

4. Some insects hide themselves by looking like:
   (a) birds and frogs
   b. leaves and twigs
   c. snow and rain

5. Scientists:
   a. live on boats
   b. know everything
   (c) look and ask questions

6. Green plants make:
   (a) oxygen   b. smog   c. sunlight

7. An ___ is a little animal with six legs.
   a. elephant   (b) insect   c. orange

8. Distance tells you:
   a. how many   b. how far   c. how old

9. An aquarium is filled with:
   (a) water   b. dirt   c. air

10. ___ breathe oxygen from the air.
    a. plants   (b) animals   c. stars

11. Some insects hide. They look like:
    (a) parts of plants   b. mice   c. Charles Darwin

12. At night a cat's pupils get:
    (a) big   b. little   c. blue

Page 100 — Energy from the Sun (Experiment)

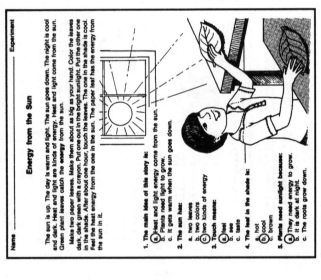

The sun is up. The day is warm and light. The sun goes down. The night is cool and dark. Heat and light are kinds of energy. The sun goes down. Green plant leaves catch the energy from the sun.

Make two paper leaves. Make them about as big as your hand. Color the leaves dark, dark green with a crayon. Put one out in the bright sunlight. Put the other one in the shade. After about one hour, touch the leaves. The one in the shade is cool. Feel the heat energy from the one in the sun. The paper leaf has the energy from the sun in it.

1. The main idea of this story is:
   (a) Heat and light energy come from the sun.
   b. Plants need light to grow.
   c. It gets warm when the sun goes down.

2. The sun has:
   a. two leaves
   (b) two colors
   c. two kinds of energy

3. Touch means:
   (a) feel
   b. see
   c. taste

4. The leaf in the shade is:
   a. hot
   (b) cool
   c. brown

5. Plants need sunlight because:
   (a) They need energy to grow.
   b. It is dark at night.
   c. The roots grow down.

Page 103 — The Cat's in the Cupboard (Experiment)

Cats hunt at night. They have eyes that can see in the dark. Look into the cat's eyes. The black part in the middle is the pupil. Put the cat in the sunlight. His pupils will get very small. Bring him back into the room. His pupils will get larger. The pupil is a hole. It lets light into the eye. Eyes need light to see. At night there is not much light. For one minute, put the cat into a closet. Take him out and look into his eyes. Now his pupils are very big. They let in all of the light they can. The cat can see in the dark.

1. The main idea of this story is:
   (a) Cats' eyes change.
   b. Cats live in closets.
   c. Cats sleep at night.

2. At night a cat's pupil:
   a. is little
   b. turns blue
   (c) is big

3. The hole that lets light in is:
   a. blue or yellow
   b. always big
   (c) the pupil

4. The cat's pupils will get small:
   (a) in the sunlight
   b. in the room
   c. in the closet

5. Cats hunt mice, so you can tell that mice come out:
   a. for recess
   (b) at night
   c. in the daytime

Page 99 — What Darwin Found (Biography)

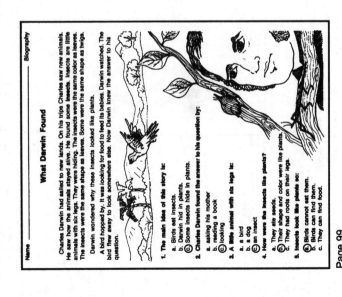

Charles Darwin had sailed to new lands. On his trips Charles saw new animals. He saw how the animals stayed alive. He found some insects. Insects are little animals with six legs. They were hiding. The insects were the same color as leaves. The insects were the same shape as leaves. Some were the same shape as twigs.

Darwin wondered why these insects looked like plants.

A bird hopped by. It was looking for food to feed its babies. Darwin watched. The bird flew away to look somewhere else. Now Darwin knew the answer to his question.

1. The main idea of this story is:
   a. Birds eat insects.
   b. Darwin hid in plants.
   (c) Some insects hide in plants.

2. Charles Darwin found the answer to his question by:
   a. asking his mother
   b. reading a book
   (c) looking

3. A little animal with six legs is:
   a. a bird
   b. a dog
   (c) an insect

4. How were the insects like plants?
   a. They ate seeds.
   (b) Their shape and color were like plants.
   c. They had roots on their legs.

5. Insects look like plants so:
   (a) Birds cannot eat them.
   b. Birds can find them.
   c. They can find food.

Page 102 — The Better to Hear You With (Experiment)

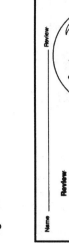

Animals with big ears can hear well. You can pretend that your ears are bigger than they are. Cup your hand behind your ear like this:

Get a long ruler and a watch that ticks. Don't let the ruler touch your ear. Put the ruler next to your ear. Move the watch away until you cannot hear it tick. Mark the place on the ruler with a piece of tape. Now try it without your hand behind your ear. Mark this distance on the ruler, too.

You will find that you can hear the watch farther away when you hold up your hand. Your hand makes your ear seem bigger. You can hear better.

1. The main idea of this story is:
   a. Animals see better at night.
   b. You can hear better at night.
   (c) Big ears help you to hear better.

2. You can hear better with your:
   a. finger in your ear
   (b) hand behind your ear
   c. hand over your eyes

3. When you find the distance, you find:
   a. how big
   (b) how far
   c. hand over your eyes

4. Find out how far away the watch is with a:
   (a) ruler
   b. gas meter
   c. meteor

5. A rabbit can hear ___ a person can.
   (a) better than
   b. the same as
   c. not as well as